The
Real Estate Agent
Redefined

The Real Estate Agent
Redefined

Jim Jaeckels

BEAVER'S
POND
PRESS

ISBN 10: 1-59298-270-0
ISBN 13: 978-1-59298-270-7

Library of Congress Catalog Number: 2008941785

Printed in the United States of America

First Printing: 2009
Second Printing: 2009

13 12 11 10 09   5 4 3 2

Cover design by Joseph Moses
Interior design and typesetting by James Monroe Design, LLC.

BEAVER'S
POND
PRESS

Beaver's Pond Press, Inc.
7104 Ohms Lane, Suite 101
Edina, MN 55439–2129
(952) 829-8818
www.BeaversPondPress.com

To order, visit www.BeaversPondBooks.com
or call 1-800-901-3480. Reseller discounts available.

This book is dedicated to my wife Nancy, daughter Mikaela, and son Charlie.

Table of Contents

Introduction

How to Redefine Yourself

The real-estate business has gone through more changes in the last three years than in the last thirty combined. Real estate sales have been redefined by 24/7 access to buyer and seller information via cell phones, PDA's, MySpace, MyBlog, You-Tube, Mobile Agent, and dozens of online services that have changed the way people think about buying and selling their homes. Agents who want to survive in an era of unprecedented change will have to thrive in an environment of truly advanced technology where quaint old tools like telephones and faxes are relics of the past.

The changes aren't just technical. With access to so much information from so many sources in so many ways, the public's attitude toward professionals has changed dramatically. Once defined by exclusive access to market information, agents built businesses by carefully doling out facts and figures according to customer needs and interests. But when data on school districts and state taxes are readily available to everyone, people aren't so sure they need real estate agents who define themselves in those terms.

Many agents take advantage of the new tools, but too many have adapted to recent changes only superficially—usually by throwing up a web site—without adequately thinking about the impact that new technologies and virtual business models have had on customer attitudes and expectations. The most important impact of new tools is the dramatic change in the competitive landscape and what those changes mean for marketing our services and positioning ourselves in the marketplace.

How is the landscape different? It's now populated with more competition than ever. In the same way that patient access to medical information has changed the medical profession and access to publishing technologies has changed the publishing industry, our own prospective customers are now doing much of the real estate agent's work themselves. They are more likely to spend several hours searching for their own homes than they are to search for an agent who seems knowledgeable and trustworthy. Proud of the information you can offer about school districts and local taxes? Thanks, but parents can go to www.schoolmatters.com and find all of the information they need about all the school districts they want in just a few minutes. You have property tax information to share? Anyone can type "property tax rate" into Google and find more relevant data than it's worth your time to offer.

New generations of home buyers and sellers are wired differently from the ones many of us have been trained to serve. Mind you, "wired differently" is already a cliché that no longer even makes sense in an increasingly wireless world; nevertheless, the concept holds true: home buyers and sellers think and act in fundamentally different ways from what they did even ten years ago. They process more information faster and with less effort than any generation before them. They're used to working in virtual environments, so they don't feel constrained by matters of time and distance. Eighty-four percent of today's homebuyers initiate their search for a home on the internet, and then find an agent to help them out.

In a wireless world, there's less time for building relationships with customers. There's less time to talk about the kids. Face-to-face interactions used to be a way to develop trust and develop long-term relationships. Those relationships often ran so deep that they were a rewarding source of repeat business. Now customers have a different attitude. They want to know what they need to know and then they're ready to move on. Results-oriented customers are all about moving on to the next thing, and they're not likely to want to spend a lot of time getting acquainted around the kitchen table.

A large number of people still have not adopted and may never adapt to the new age of technology and communication: the senior segment of the population.

Perceptions inside and outside our industry are further redefining our roles and opportunities for success. The perception that real estate agents get rich off of inflated commissions attracts tens of thousands of new agents per year. At the same time, low barriers to entry for new agents are eroding the status of the profession. "For Sale by Owner" (FSBO) shops and discount brokers reinforce the notion that if you can steam a mirror, you can buy or sell real estate. True or not, those perceptions drive down commissions and drive up the attitude that our services are overpriced and overrated.

Organizations outside our industry are essentially fishing upstream to capture leads on post-purchase surveys to determine who is interested in real estate services. These companies then contact real estate brokers and dangle the prospects under their noses, saying, "I have a list of prospects who have indicated they are buying or selling a home in the near future. I can provide you with the list, but I want a 30% referral fee." These prospects may eventually come to agents anyway, yet there's always a chance that someone else will buy the leads from the upstream companies and leave you empty handed.

What do these redefining factors mean for you? They mean ideas like "communications strategy," "relationship building," "sales and marketing strategy," "prospecting," "competition," and a host of other concepts have to be defined and redefined, too.

What's the answer?

When surveyed, clients say that saving time, saving money, and reducing stress are the most important goals they have for the buying and selling process. People have too much to do and too little time. They crave professional assistance that takes at least some of the stress out of the buying and selling transaction. The National Association of Realtors television ad says it best: "Real estate agents have a job so you can have a life."

To meet customer expectations, you can redefine yourself by reinvesting in your knowledge base, your research strategies, your relationship building, your network, and your tool set. You can do it by taking IT classes and attending personal training and development programs to market and brand yourself more effectively. You can incorporate a professional selling process into your presentation to make sure you communicate efficiently and clearly. And you can read industry newsletters on market trends so you are on top of the information that clients need before they know they need it.

Information may be free and easy to access, but agents who know how to use information, where to find the right information, and how to evaluate and interpret it bring value to clients. Do-it-yourself clients are not trained, experienced professionals, and they won't always know what information means, whether it's reliable, or how it might help them predict the outcome of a transaction. That's where you come in. Clients may be able to find data on their own, but they don't know how to use it in negotiations. That's where you build value—and trust. By helping your clients recognize what they don't know before they realize they don't know it, you'll go a long way toward redefining your relationships, building trust, and building business.

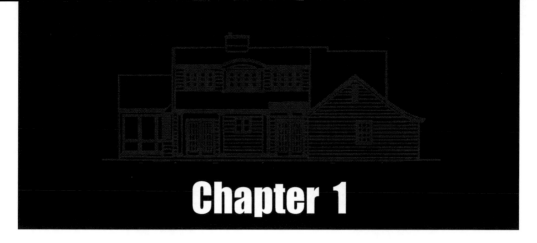

Chapter 1

It's a Lifestyle with a Purpose

---

*"People are afraid of the future, of the unknown.
If a man faces up to it, and takes the dare of the future,
he can have some control over his destiny.
That is an exciting idea to me, better than waiting with
everybody else to see what is going to happen."*

—John H. Glenn Jr.

All anybody who wants to be a real estate agent has to do is be eighteen years old, take a class for a month, take a test for three hours, and pay $1,200. Unlike professionals in engineering, medicine, accounting, and law—where the upfront educational and financial commitment is substantial—the professional real estate agent needs slightly more than a pulse to qualify. That's right: steam a mirror and you're in.

As a result of low barriers to entry, real estate agents have been characterized as back-slapping, country club, part-time hobbyists who drive expensive cars, wine and dine clients, and make tons of money. They have everything but respect.

Barriers to entry in real estate are low, and that makes competition fierce. Barriers to information are almost nonexistent, so investment in yourself is essential to keeping competitive. Agents must develop business acumen, selling skills, and technical know-how. An agent must have a business plan, set goals, and study up on industry trends, must research in ways that bring true value to the consumer. Information isn't enough. You have to provide knowledge—even wisdom to truly serve your clients. Your job is to get to the center of the transaction and stay there.

> *Barriers to entry in real estate are low, and that makes competition fierce.*

Real estate is not a job. It is not a career. It's a lifestyle. If you plan to be successful, chances are you will eat, breathe, and sleep this business. It is not a 9-to-5 job. The business knows no hours. You work when you work and play when you play—and sometimes the two intersect. Monday mornings and Friday nights mean little because your week tends neither to start nor stop.

No activity level or skill set can replace the need for a passion for people and homes. You can possess all of the work ethic and skill in the world, but if you cannot get people to like and trust you up front, you won't get a chance to use all those wonderful abilities.

Independence is one of the greatest advantages of being an agent. As long as you perform legally, morally, and ethically, and stay within company and industry standards, you can run your business exactly the way you want. You are free to let your creativity and work ethic take you where you want to go.

Your income potential has no ceiling. It is extremely rewarding to know that the more and better you perform, the more you can earn—which is unlike many other careers. The older you get in the real estate business, the more you are appreciated for your experience, wisdom, and tenure.

The agent's lifestyle is guided by intense time pressures. You're always on call, and you're always expected to be accessible. In a typical corporate setting, if you call a client back within the same day, that is good service. In real estate, if you don't call clients back within an hour they think you don't care.

In real estate, if you don't call clients back within an hour they think you don't care.

The lifestyle is subject to dramatic fluctuations in income, and the ups and downs demand a system and discipline for managing money. It is not uncommon to make $40,000 in one month and then to make nothing for the next three. Annual ups and downs can be even more severe. You may go big one year and clip coupons the next.

You can take several steps to smooth out the bumps. When you redefine yourself in terms of the real estate lifestyle, you structure your days and weeks with new purpose:

- ✔ Uphold a client-centered 24/7 work ethic
- ✔ Conduct service-driven research
- ✔ Gain new knowledge
- ✔ Grow your network
- ✔ Develop and refine your negotiation skills
- ✔ Manage your money with discipline
- ✔ Persevere in the face of daily challenges
- ✔ Work independently *and* with others
- ✔ Follow through on behalf of your clients

✔ Maintain self-discipline and self-motivation

✔ Work hard *consistently*

✔ Develop your marketing aptitude (personal and business promotion)

✔ Sustain your self-confidence

✔ Sharpen your listening and presentation skills

✔ Know the strengths and limitations of your psychological type

✔ Be a caregiver

✔ Manage your time profitably for yourself and your clients

✔ Stay current with technology trends

✔ Become an employee recruiter/trainer/developer

✔ Develop organizational tools and processes

A real estate agent who wants not only to survive but thrive in today's marketplace must *focus on what you know in addition to who you know*.

To thrive in today's marketplace, you must focus on what you know in addition to who you know.

This book will assist you in providing pinnacle client service. It is meant to give new meaning to the words, "a by referral only, full-service real estate agent for life!" Whether you are new to the business of real estate or a veteran, this book can help you grow your business by using a technology- and client-based philosophy.

Even if you are the hardest working and most skilled real estate agent in the industry, you must sincerely and passionately demonstrate concern for your client's best interests. If you don't, you will miss the boat over and over and watch your business sail away.

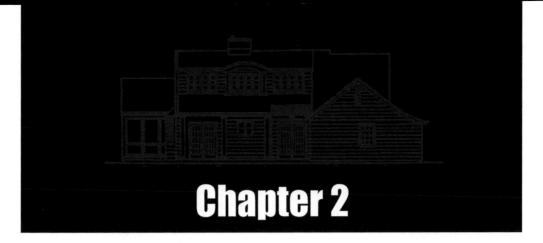

Chapter 2

It's a Business with a Plan and a Position

"If you don't know where you are going,
any road will get you there."

—Lewis Carroll

The best place to begin in business is with a business plan and goal setting. Planning business activities and defining goals helps you determine a course of action that provides direction and focus. Whether you set short-term goals or long-term goals, what makes goals effective is that they are attainable, measurable, and memorable.

Having a business with a position means staking out territory in the minds of your prospects so they perceive you in very specific ways. That is, your business plan may be for a real estate company, but your position is how you want to be perceived by your prospective customers.

Position is how you want to be perceived by your prospective customers.

Goals Redefined

Long-term goals are achieved by dividing them up into short- and medium-range goals annually, quarterly, monthly, weekly, or even hourly. But long, short, day, month, minute, week—whatever your goals—you better have your sights set on positive cash flow or you can kiss your sweet assumptions about making a living in real estate good-bye.

Goal-setting tools for this section are included in the appendix.

Exhibit A: long-term goals.

- ✔ Retirement planning: Retire by age 60.
- ✔ Create extra earnings: Own residential properties that provide income whether you work or not in residential sales.
- ✔ Networking is the key: Become a "rainmaker" whereby you generate business through your relationships while others service the client.

Larger, visionary goals that take months or years to achieve typically dictate what interim goals to set. For example, if you want to own your first investment property in three years, you will have to earn specific amounts on an on-going basis each quarter. To reach your quarterly goals, set an immediate goal of taking a course on real estate investment to educate yourself on rental properties.

Goal-Setting Redefined: Long-Term Goals (3 or more years)

	Critical Goals	Value of Goals	Current Status	Critical Action
1				
2				
3				
4				
5				

Exhibit B provides you with an annual plan.

- ✔ Hire an assistant
- ✔ Hire a buyer's agent
- ✔ Earn $200,000 annual gross income
- ✔ Develop a corporate image and marketing campaign

Exhibit C is a quarterly plan.

- ✔ Send out spring mailer to sphere group
- ✔ Close the clients on the books
- ✔ Learn the latest company technology advancements

Exhibit D is a daily to-do list.

Having the boxes in front of each goal keeps tasks from becoming overwhelming and engenders a feeling of accomplishment when you check them off.

- ✔ Mail prospecting letters
- ✔ Write and mail a monthly newsletter
- ✔ Call clients daily to touch base

Exhibit B

Goal-Setting Redefined: One-Year Goals			
Critical Goals	Value of Goals	Current Status	Critical Action
1			
2			
3			
4			
5			

Exhibit C

Goal-Setting Redefined: Quarterly			
Critical Goals	Value of Goals	Current Status	Critical Action
1			
2			
3			
4			
5			

Goal-Setting Redefined: Weekly

Critical Goals	Value of Goals	Current Status	Critical Action
1			
2			
3			
4			
5			

Exhibit D

Daily To-Do List

Name

#		✔	#		✔
1			21		
2			22		
3			23		
4			24		
5			25		
6			26		
7			27		
8			28		
9			29		
10			30		
11			31		
12			32		
13			33		
14			34		
15			35		
16			36		
17			37		
18			38		
19			39		
20			40		

Break goals into manageable tasks

If your sales goal for the month is twelve units and you are at three units in week two, don't focus on the nine units you have left to sell. That can cause stress and pressure that can spill over onto the customers you are depending on for sales. Instead, focus on the daily tasks that will get you to the next sale. Make ten sales calls, send 300 mailers to your sphere group, and hold two Open Houses. Pace yourself. Checking off your daily list of tasks gives you a feeling of accomplishment and reinforces a positive attitude.

Just as you would develop habits, disciplines, goals, and a schedule to physically train your body for a marathon, setting daily, weekly, monthly, and annual goals for yourself and your business will exercise and develop your mind to function instinctively for new growth. Your goals help you work more efficiently and effectively.

Business Planning

Once you establish your goals, especially the initial long-term visionary ones, a business plan is essential. A good business plan is comprised of the following parts:

- ✔ Mission statement
- ✔ Product/service offerings
- ✔ Sales/marketing plans
- ✔ Operations/systems/distribution plans
- ✔ Target market definition
- ✔ Technology needs

✔ Financial needs

✔ Management/employee needs

Mission Statement

Create a mission statement that captures the reason for your existence. It can be as simple as, "To become the leading real estate agent in the country based on volume of sales" or "To provide premier representation services to the clients and market that I serve." Here's an example:

My mission as a professional real estate agent is to provide buyers and sellers with superior representation services. My goal is to maximize the value of every transaction for my clients, and I measure my success by customer satisfaction with my efforts.

Product/Service Offering

In real estate, you are the product or service, and your reputation is what people value. Your company offers products and programs for the client, and it is critical that you take advantage of those, especially in a full-service, value-added approach to the business. But the client is still hiring *you.* You and your level of expertise are inseparable, so it's being aware of trends, markets, and properties that will enable you to project the level of expertise that consumers are looking for. So build research and study into your business plan. Invest in technologies that provide connectivity with clients and service providers

In real estate, you are the product or service and your reputation is what people value.

because of the time it saves you and the access it gives you. Although consumers will have access to information, they won't necessarily know where to find or be able to access it as quickly as you as long as you have the right tools. In addition, taking classes and reading books on negotiation strategies, selling and marketing strategies, and home construction are critical in keeping you sharp and on top of the industry.

Sales/Marketing Plans

Who you are matters, but what you do matters, too, and what you have to do well is sell. Selling is the skill you use to ultimately make your business take off. When developing a business plan, these two broad activities—being an expert and selling expertly—can be used to develop the plan and then monitor it. One of the reasons that writing a business plan is so valuable is that the process forces you to prioritize all your activities—the broad ones and the narrowly defined ones. By drafting a plan and making decisions about which customers to pursue and which activities are best suited to pursuing them, you will be able to accurately produce strategies and tactics for growing your business.

Analyze "activity types" to optimize sales

The following is a list of activities you'll typically conduct to obtain business:

- ✔ Open houses
- ✔ Sphere and client direct-mail marketing
- ✔ Volunteering
- ✔ Strategic alliances with lenders, accountants, trust departments, etc.

✔ Door-to-door knocking

✔ Getting involved in schools or religious organizations

✔ Networking with family and friends

✔ Keeping in touch with past clients in person or on the phone

✔ Calling on expired listings

✔ Calling on "For Sale by Owner" Shops

✔ Holding client appreciation parties

✔ Niche marketing

Assign goals for each activity

Attainable, measurable, memorable goals look something like this:

✔ Hold two Open Houses per weekend for the next three months.

✔ Mail new listings or a newsletter once a month to my clients and sphere group.

✔ Be involved with one organization I believe in by the end of the year.

✔ Hold one annual client appreciation party in the summer.

The second part of the equation is not on **what you do** like above, but rather on **how well you do it**, or your skill set at each of the activities.

The following is a list of "competency areas:"

✔ Listing presentation

✔ Buyer presentation

✔ Purchase agreement offer presentation (one with multiple offers, one not)

✔ Receiving of an offer presentation (one with multiple offers, one not)

✔ Holding an Open House

✔ When direct mailing, the quality of materials and message reflects a skill set

✔ Your relationship with your schools, religious groups, and volunteer organizations

Like in most sales situations, once you have a history of performance with regard to this plan, you can almost forecast sales for the coming year. For example, if for every Open House you can pick up two buyers and close those buyers at a 50 percent close ratio, and you want to make ten sales a year from Open Houses —you will have to hold 20 Open Houses. Once you have a formula like this worked out, you can determine how much money you want to make and back into the numbers based on activity and skill set levels.

The activity and skill sets are often dependent on the target market you are trying to serve. The following is a list of audiences to target:

✔ Seniors

✔ Downsizing market

✔ First time home-buyers

✔ Transitional, upward mobility people

✔ Luxury market clientele

✔ A specific geographic area

✔ Alternative lifestyle market

✔ Clients based upon bilingual language ability

✔ Relocation clients

✔ Condominium market

✔ Hobby Farm market

✔ Investment properties

✔ Lake properties

How you market and sell to each of these distinct market segments is uniquely different, and becoming the specialist in each market requires a specific approach, strategy, and mindset.

Additional elements of your business plan

✔ Implement a self-coaching plan. Programs designed to help you reach your full potential personally or professionally help you set goals and plan your business. Programs help you focus on what you do best and get rid of the rest while differentiating you from other agents.

✔ Go to work during working hours. You gain flexibility and freedom through focus. To maintain focus on sales and service, you must maintain a discipline of going into the office to work. This is of critical importance in the real estate business where business and personal activities threaten to break focus throughout the day.

Implement a self-coaching plan.

✔ Mail and e-mail new listings to your sphere group of contacts. Letting your clients know when you get a new listing or sell a property accomplishes two things: you tell them that you are on top of the market and that you are working to promote your properties.

✔ Stay current on relevant technologies. The business is always changing. Your clients have to keep up, and they expect you to as well.

✔ Take continuing education classes throughout the year. Time your continuing education to avoid spending beautiful summer days in a classroom for 7.5 hours.

✔ Get involved in volunteer organizations. Find organizations and causes that you are truly interested in and join them. It is a way of expanding your network while making a fruitful contribution to something that matters. Volunteering puts you in continuous contact with people who get to know and trust you as a professional.

✔ Implement a neighborhood website. Create a neighborhood website to promote yourself and others who are involved with it. Make it a one-stop website for goods and services. Place your branding contact information on every page. For a Web resource that can help you build your neighborhood network, visit www.connectingneighbors.com.

✔ Stay in touch with top referral sources. Call or meet with them in person. Mailers and e-mails are not sufficient because they don't build rapport. It takes face-to-face or voice-to-voice contact, which is the most productive and cost-effective way of getting referrals anyway.

✔ Create strategic alliances. Many referral sources have the trust and attention of clients and people who are potential clients for you. These include bank trust departments, mortgage lenders, attorneys, accountants, and dozens of other service providers.

✔ Adhere to buying/listing checklist. As a matter of organization and follow through, keep on top of client tracking systems. The low investment of time pays off in higher productivity. Most agents have to set time aside to track progress because the step requires concentration to be effective.

✔ Read e-mails and periodicals from National Association of Realtors (NAR) and your local and state associations. This is one of the best ways to stay on top of the market, industry, and your business in general.

✔ Send market update information. The general public has access to information, but the real estate agent knows how to interpret and evaluate it. Don't just send information because if clients feel they could have dug that up themselves, you risk reinforcing the idea that clients don't need agents. Tell them what the information *means*, how to use it. And every now and then point out information that's not accurate as a warning that there's a lot of information out there that can be misleading.

✔ Listings at 7%. There is no easier way to give yourself a raise than charging what you are worth.

✔ Extreme control of business expenses. The old saying, "It's not what you earn but what you spend that can make or break you." In a career where the income is sporadic and inconsistent it is critical to have a close control on spending and money management both business- and personal-wise.

✔ Implement and maintain Quicken. Using this or any other money management tool is key to managing the finances.

✔ Develop a marketing plan up front and stick to it. A regular and consistent marketing campaign to attract clients is important. Having a pro-active game plan as to what and when things will be sent makes for better control of the business and helps to alleviate ebbs and flows of business production and sales.

✔ Do Open Houses on a regular basis. There is no less expensive way or productive way to sell your clients home or attain buyers than to work an Open House. The cost of doing the Open House is virtually free, and you have ready, willing, and able buyers coming through the door. The added exposure is great in working to sell the home for the seller.

✔ Ask for the business. Never assume that just because you are in the business that people assume you are in the market for new clients. There may be a perception that you are either too busy or too successful and don't need the business. Simply say, "I could use your help. I am looking to grow my business and wanted you to know I would both value and enjoy the opportunity to assist you or anyone you know with a real estate transaction."

✔ What message is being sent and how? You are the product/ service offering. How you present yourself, brand yourself, market yourself, and so on is critical to the direct end result of your business success.

✔ Don't rely too much on written communication. Use the telephone. The best way to build rapport and make your mark in your sphere's mind is to have actual dialogues with them, not one-way communication.

✔ Work less, earn more, and find balance in your life! You are no good to your clients without first taking care of yourself. By implementing the right strategies and systems for efficiency and effectiveness you will actually find yourself working less and earning more money.

Variables to Success

✔ Work ethic

✔ People skills

✔ Ability to network

✔ Negotiation skills

✔ Money management discipline

✔ Perseverance

✔ Ability to work independently or with others

✔ Follow-through

✔ Self-discipline and self-motivation

✔ Marketing aptitude (personal and business promotion)

✔ Self-confidence

✔ Listening and presentation skills

✔ Having a care-giver personality

✔ Time manager

✔ Perform technological tasks

✔ Employee recruiter/trainer/developer

✔ Organization skills

THE BUSINESS PLAN

❏ Implement the Real Estate Agent Redefined!

❏ Go to work/office during working hours.

❏ Mail and e-mail to sphere new listings.

❏ Stay current on all technology.

❏ Take continuing education courses as needed in a timely manner.

❏ Get involved with Kreuz und Quer, French Immersion, Hockey, School Carnival, Car Driving and other volunteer opportunities.

❏ Implement Richmond Hills News Program.

❏ Stay in touch with top referral sources.

❏ Set up strategic alliances.

❏ Adhere to listing/buying checklist and keep systems up.

❏ Read e-mails from MAR, and NAR.

❏ Send market update information.

❏ Listings at 7.0%.

❏ Extreme control of business expenses.

❏ Implement and maintain Quicken.

❏ Develop marketing plan upfront and stick to it.

❏ Do Open Houses on a regular basis.

❏ Ask for the business.

❏ What message is being sent and how?

❏ Don't rely so much on written communication. Use the phone.

❏ Work less, earn more, MAINTAIN BALANCE IN MY LIFE!

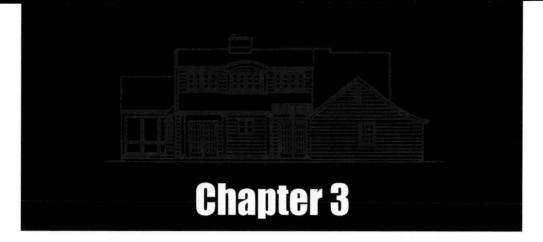

Chapter 3

It's an Office Designed for Sales

"Let all things be descent and in order."
—Corinthians 14:40

To be the best that you can be at capturing new business and developing a revenue stream, your day-to-day administrative details must be in place to support you. Your options are do all your administrative tasks yourself, hire an assistant, or come up with an alternative. Doing it all yourself—including answering phones, stamping envelopes, and filing—is not productive use of your time. Hiring an assistant is costly. But a hybrid system of doing some of the work yourself and ***outsourcing*** support functions to maximize productivity can lead to the business growth you're looking for.

No one is equally skilled in sales, organization, prospecting, showing, marketing, lead generation, closing, time management, and all the rest. The key is to determine what your abilities and skills are, perform only those on a daily basis, and outsource the rest to others.

There's skill, there's love, and there's money

Deciding how to structure your office and your workday requires reflection about the work you have to do, the work you like to do, the work that brings in money, the work that costs money, and the work you couldn't do well even if someone paid you. To begin thinking about these important questions, I've devised the exercise that follows. To begin, write down all the tasks, responsibilities, and jobs that you perform on a daily basis.

Here is a sample list:

- ✔ Put stamps on envelopes
- ✔ Set up inspections
- ✔ Prospect
- ✔ Send mailers
- ✔ Do listing and buyer presentations
- ✔ Take photos of your listings
- ✔ Call/e-mail for showing follow-up
- ✔ Handle phone calls and e-mails
- ✔ Negotiate transaction
- ✔ Put together marketing pieces
- ✔ Turn in files

Label each item according to the following qualities:

- ✔ Tasks that you are good at, love to do, and are paid for. **Example:** meeting with someone to bring them on as a client.
- ✔ Tasks that you are good at or love to do, but are not paid to do.

Activity Redefined

Name:

Think about the daily activities you perform in a typical week and list them below. Include large and small tasks such as attending meetings, answering e-mails, making sales calls, opening the mail, delegating tasks to others, and so on. Be as detailed and comprehensive as possible.

1		21	
2		22	
3		23	
4		24	
5		25	
6		26	
7		27	
8		28	
9		29	
10		30	
11		31	
12		32	
13		33	
14		34	
15		35	
16		36	
17		37	
18		38	
19		39	
20		40	

Example: writing and designing my marketing material, i.e., listing brochures.

✔ Tasks that you are good at, do not love to do, and don't get paid for.

Example: setting up appointments for inspections and appraisals

✔ Tasks that you are not good at, don't love to do, and don't get paid for.

Example: fixing my computer when it is down

With this information, you know where to begin thinking about outsourcing and taking advantage of businesses that make a living doing what you can't do, don't like to do, or shouldn't be doing because it drains energy and resources away from serving customers and growing sales.

Hire photography and virtual tour services, sign companies, brochure companies, and administrative personnel who work on a per-hour contract basis so you don't have to hire an employee and take on all the extra work that having too many employees can entail.

To combat the loss of control, it is essential that you maintain strong focus and discipline.

The following list shows how you can delegate or outsource specific tasks so you can focus attention on customers, prospects, and sales.

In this business, it is easy to allow your business to control you instead of you controlling the business. To combat the loss of control, it is essential that you maintain strong focus and discipline.

One way to do that is to determine when the best time is to do each activity.

The following is a weekly itinerary that has worked well for many agents.

Monday

- ✔ Catch up from weekend
- ✔ Do client weekly activity reports
- ✔ Update "clients in process"
- ✔ Schedule broker opens
- ✔ Provide market analysis of last week's activity
- ✔ Provide recap of last week's activity and results and a game plan for the coming week

Tuesday

- ✔ 9–10 sales meeting
- ✔ Tour of real estate agent Open Houses
- ✔ Set up Open Houses for the weekend

Wednesday

- ✔ Make sure Open House ads are right
- ✔ Forward e-mail networking items to buyers
- ✔ Four-color picture ads

Thursday

- ✔ 9–10 exceptional properties meetings
- ✔ Make sure four-color picture ad is right

Friday/daily

- ✔ Sync cell phone to computer
- ✔ Take care of e-mails and voice mails
- ✔ Check buyer/seller checklists
- ✔ Handle scheduling of inspections, appraisals, showings
- ✔ Keep up "to-do" list
- ✔ Turn in files
- ✔ Set up client searches
- ✔ Learn technology
- ✔ Order virtual tours, VHT
- ✔ Set up showings
- ✔ Order closing gifts
- ✔ Handle faxes
- ✔ Update lists
- ✔ Fax cover sheets
- ✔ Buyer/seller binders
- ✔ Listing/buying checklist
- ✔ Home selling process
- ✔ Pricing guidelines
- ✔ Marketing your property
- ✔ Marketing campaign
- ✔ Houses before the sign goes up
- ✔ Produce vinyl packets
- ✔ Listing paperwork packets

Abilities Redefined

Real Estate Agent's Redefined Abilities

- [ ] Listing presentation
- [ ] Buyer presentation
- [ ] Offer presentation/reception
- [ ] Negotiation
- [ ] Representation
- [ ] Preparation
- [ ] Socialization
- [ ] Evaluation
- [ ] Showings
- [ ] Counsel/consult
- [ ] Be visionary
- [ ] Closings

Real Estate Agent/Associate Responsibilities

- [ ] Cover Jim during time off
- [ ] Design brochures

Assistant/Associate Activities

- [ ] Handle scheduling, inspections, appraisals, changes
- [ ] Follow up with sales to assure on course for closing
- [ ] Schedule Open Houses and broker's opens
- [ ] Order virtual tours
- [ ] Copy and turn in files
- [ ] Schedule closings
- [ ] Communicate via voice mail and e-mail
- [ ] Contact letters
- [ ] Set up initial custom searches and send them out

- [ ] Listen and communicate
- [ ] Design marketing pieces
- [ ] Problem solve
- [ ] Handle hurdles that require client contact/consultation
- [ ] Stay in constant contact with client between consummation and closing
- [ ] Develop team
- [ ] CMA'S
- [ ] Maintain systems and office organization
- [ ] Continually update and improve marketing to sphere of influence
- [ ] Communicate via voice mail and e-mail
- [ ] Create and maintain file flow system (Board in Office)

- [ ] Website development
- [ ] Develop brochure box flyers
- [ ] Develop moving address post cards
- [ ] Monthly mailers, labels, and stamps

- [ ] Send out daily new listings, prices changes, back on market
- [ ] Schedule Star Tribune/Pioneer Press ads
- [ ] Set up showings
- [ ] Build binders
- [ ] Mail necessary items
- [ ] Listing/buyer checklist folders
- [ ] Update lists
- [ ] Prepare folders for new listing to go in home
- [ ] Send weekly feedback forms to sellers with what we have done to sell home
- [ ] Keep client files in order
- [ ] Prepare buyer/seller packets

Finally, find products and services that cater to the real estate business and put them to work to streamline your operation and optimize productivity:

✔ Sign companies

✔ Designers and printers of marketing materials

✔ Virtual tour companies

✔ Accountants and bookkeepers

✔ Attorneys

✔ Website designers

✔ Administrative assistants

✔ Printing companies

*Streamline your operation
and optimize productivity.*

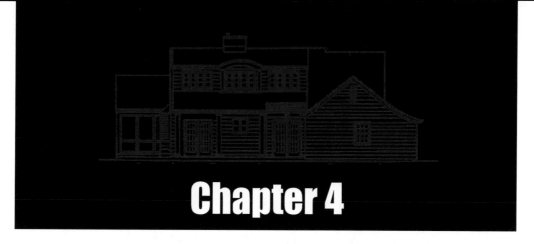

Chapter 4

It's a Business Built on Referrals

"To be trusted is a greater compliment than to be loved."

—George McDonald

You can generate new business in all kinds of ways. One way is to have an extensive and expensive marketing campaign that requires a lot of direct mail and mass advertising. Though reaching a larger number of people, this method requires a large investment of time, systems, and money. It's not clear that the pay offs justify the costs, and it's easy to make a lot of expensive mistakes before you discover strategies and tactics that work.

A better option is to implement a referral-based business strategy in which you identify a limited and targeted audience, such as the people who know you and with whom you already have a relationship, and determine ways of reaching them with your key messages. This book is dedicated to the latter because it's the most cost-effective method for growing your business. The advertising/scattershot approach is costly, time-consuming, and risky for lots of reasons.

One is that direct mail eats up time and resources many agents just don't have. But the referral-based business approach optimizes the return on one thing every agent has the most of and must invest anyway: time.

Top Ten Secrets to Marketing a Successful Referral-based Business

1. Develop systems of organization, logistics, and incentives for running a referral-based business. When you work on a referral basis, you must let everyone you meet know what you do and how well you do it. Provide incentives for everyone—including your spouse or significant other—to refer you within their sphere of influence.

   To ensure that your office is set up to maximize referrals, you need simple, fast, and easy ways to collect information about prospective customers: name, address, e-mail, phone, cell, and web address.

2. Develop a marketing and sales strategy designed for a referral-based business. Design a corporate identity that explains your unique value as an agent and why others should refer you to friends, colleagues, and others. If you work for a large brand-name company, incorporate its brand identity into yours so you are aligned in the customer's mind with the well-known company.

   As part of your strategy, incorporate the same branding into your

Your unique image differentiates you from other real estate agents' boilerplate images.

website. Your unique image differentiates you from other real estate agents' boilerplate images.

3. Align yourself with real estate agents who may be too busy to handle all the work that comes their way. It may take some time to get referrals from other agents, but you stand to learn a lot from the relationships while gaining their trust.

4. When working with clients, be pro-active in educating them about the buying or selling process so they feel empowered and in control. When you reduce a client's stress, you increase a client's trust in you.

5. Develop a newsletter that gives new homeowners valuable information and keeps you top of mind when someone asks your customer to recommend a good real estate agent.

6. Develop and maintain a "business resource directory" to assist your clients with names of people who can help them with products and services that are complementary to your own. List businesses that will help them make improvements to their homes such as contractors like tilers, plumbers, framers, painters, and business service professionals like attorneys, accountants, or financial planners. These are all people from whom you can receive referrals as well.

At the same time, develop strategic alliances with referral sources such as trust departments, lenders and mortgage bankers, attorneys, accountants, financial planners, and employment/recruiter agencies. Align yourself with relocation companies, apartment guide agencies, and businesses that may be relocating people to your city. Join volunteer organizations that you are truly passionate about. Anyone you develop an ongoing relationship with gets added to your sphere of influence list, i.e., like your dry cleaner, dentist, or doctor.

Develop strategic alliances with referral sources such as trust departments, lenders and mortgage bankers, attorneys, accountants, financial planners, and employment/recruiter agencies.

Here's an example:

Endorsement List

This is a preface to let you know that as a matter of disclaimer, I have had great experiences with the following people. Though I endorse them whole-heartedly, I do not take responsibility or liability for them.

Accountants

Dan Morrison
555.935.5935

Architects

Tom McIver
555.904.1332

Auto Body

Fender Kraft
555.546.7094

Albert Auto Body
555.558.0107

Home Improvement

Basement Water Proofing
555.537.4849

Boiler Removal
555.537.2014

Ace Inspection

Bob
555.361.0270

Cabinetry and Plumbing Fixtures

Big Value Stores

Carpet Installations

Jeff Dallas
555.343.0440

Carpet and Upholstery Cleaning

Kathleen
555.780.0505

Carpenters

John Swift
555.722.4983

Paul Solder
555.936.9983

7. Create professionally designed marketing pieces that introduce your new real estate career to your sphere group. Explain how the skills, abilities, and personality traits that made you successful in your previous career are applicable to a referral-based real estate business. Produce it on a four-color, double-sided, heavy coated stock with significant size to catch attention.

A note on color: When I used red and black, my average transaction was $230,000. I switched to gold, black, and white and my average sale doubled because I began attracting higher-end clients who equated the colors with classier business practices.

Sample brochure copy introducing your new venture:

Dear Family, Friends, and Business Associates

Greetings! I'm proud to announce a new venture that combines my fifteen years of corporate experience in sales, marketing, and management with my love of homes: residential real-estate sales.

As I take this leap of faith, I move confidently ahead knowing that my past success was built on a referral-based business.

Beginning in January, I will be aligning myself with one of the nation's best real estate companies. If I can be of assistance to you or anyone you know considering the purchase or sale of a home or any real-estate-related matters, please know that I would value and enjoy the opportunity to work with you.

A formal business card announcement is forthcoming!

Follow up with your recipient list to ask if they have received the announcement and to support you by offering names of others to whom you can offer your services.

8. Conduct post-closing follow-up. Following up is a key to building rapport for the future. Call to see how the move-in went. If you've ever received a follow-up call from a doctor's office to see how you're feeling, you know what a favorable impression such a call can make. When someone asks your clients where to find a good real estate agent, they'll remember your call and pass your name along.

9. At your initial meeting with clients, provide a customized folder for their records. In the pouch have agency and non-discrimination disclosures, a business card magnet so they know how to find you, a personalized notepad/writing tablet, and a calendar.

10. Meet with your broker/manager to determine a business plan of activities and skills that will optimize growth based on referrals. Your manager will be able to lend some perspective to your plans and help you avoid wasting resources on strategies that aren't suited to your goals. Discuss niche markets and which ones are most likely to be growth opportunities.

Referrals Redefined				Strategic Alliances		
	Name	Best Results			Name		
1				21			
2				22			
3				23			
4				24			
5				25			
6				26			
7				27			
8				28			
9				29			
10				30			
11				31			
12				32			
13				33			
14				34			
15				35			
16				36			
17				37			
18				38			
19				39			
20				40			

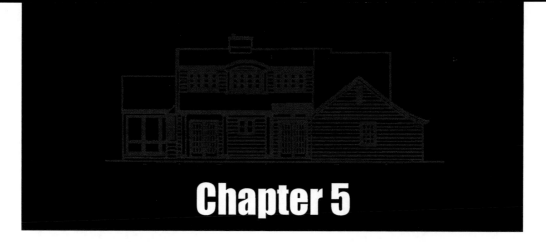

Chapter 5

It's a Selling Process that Doesn't Really End

"The most successful people I've known are the ones who do more listening than talking."

—Bernard Baruch

This chapter offers the greatest opportunity for you to set yourself apart from others by explaining how to incorporate a tested selling process focused on customer needs and desires before, during, and after each presentation. One of the challenges of achieving excellence in selling is that many agents believe they already know a process and use it as well as they can. Another challenge is that many people think the selling process starts and stops during the sales presentation, while in front of the client. In fact, what you do before and after your time in front of the customer is equally important. For example, if you get a referral from a friend, spending time to thank your friend for the referral is very important—not only because it is courteous, but because it gives you a chance to learn more about the referral. You may learn whether the referral is interviewing multiple agents—or is buying, selling, or transitioning—all of which helps prepare for your face-to-face time with your referral. It also demonstrates to the referral source how you do business: when you courteously and professionally follow up to thank them for the referral, they're likely to refer you again in the future.

When contacting prospective clients, do it at a time and place where they are most likely to be attentive. Also, ask if it is a good time, to show that you respect their time. Before picking up the phone, make a list of rapport-building questions and answers. The dialogue usually sounds like this:

Agent: Hi, this is Mary Smith with XYZ Real Estate and your name was provided to me by a mutual friend, John Jones. Are you in the middle of anything, or is this a good time to talk? [People appreciate your professionalism when you respect their time, and you gain their undivided attention if it is indeed a good time to talk.]

Prospect: Yes, I have a few minutes.

Agent: I understand that you are looking to sell your home. I would value and enjoy the opportunity to help you out. How can I be of service to you?

If a client is purchasing a home, your office is a good place to meet. All of the resources you'll need will be available, it's a professional atmosphere, and your client is away from distractions.

When clients are selling or transitioning, it is a good idea to meet at their home so you can see it. When setting the appointment at a seller's home, try to set a meeting time that will give you their undivided attention.

The best place to conduct business is around the kitchen table because clients are usually most comfortable there. But as usual, never assume—ask clients where they would prefer to talk. Once that is established, confirm the time frame for your meeting so they know you respect their time. It is also a good idea to explain up front the itinerary for the meeting so they know what to expect.

Confirm the time frame for your meeting so they know you respect their time.

The seven-step selling process

Step One: Build rapport and establish common ground

In this step, you ask questions to remove hurdles and establish that you are interested in your client's goals.

Agent: Though I would like to cover several important points with you this evening, more than anything, the goal for me is to find out what your goals are, so when you walk out of here this evening, your questions will have been addressed and you feel comfortable with me, my company, and the process.

Client: We want to know what purchasing a home is all about.

Agent: By the end of the meeting, we will have covered the entire home-buying process so you're comfortable with the process. How does that sound?

Step Two: Determine clients' wants and needs and the why

At this point in the presentation, ask permission to ask more detailed questions. This accomplishes two things: one, the client can tell through your questioning that you are truly interested in their best interests, not your own. And two, you find out what you want to know from them.

Agent: To determine how I can best explain the home-buying process to you, do you mind if I ask a few questions?

Client: Feel free to ask questions.

Agent: [Typical questions include—]

- ✔ What has been your experience in purchasing a home?
- ✔ What have you done so far?
- ✔ How do you feel going into this?
- ✔ Have you seen any homes yet?
- ✔ What are you looking for in a home?
- ✔ How do you feel I can best help you?
- ✔ Have you met with a lender?
- ✔ What else would you like to know?

Follow up each answer with "Why?" to get them to elaborate and to ensure you understand their motives and feelings.

When appropriate, follow up each answer with "Why?" to get them to elaborate and to ensure you understand their motives and feelings related to the buying or selling process. While they are answering this, make notes so you can go back and address each item and let them know you are listening.

For example, my wife and I had just had our first child and she had been house ridden for about three to four days. One sunny day, my wife says, "I am hungry for Asian food. Let's drive down to that restaurant in Northfield." (An hour's drive from the Twin Cities). Feeling like it would take more time than I wanted to devote to getting lunch, I replied, "There are plenty of good Asian restaurants right here in the Twin Cities. Why don't we just go to one of those?" She asked me to pull the car over and began in her post partum demeanor to emphatically persist to go to the one in Northfield while I remained strong on a local restaurant. She finally came out and said, "I have cabin fever and am sick of being stuck in a home with all of this beautiful weather. I don't really care if we go to that Asian restaurant or not, I just need to go for a long ride away from home." End of conversation, lesson learned, off to Northfield we went.

Step Three: Establish belief and trust

Use open-ended questions so the client does most of the talking. Keep the emphasis on your clients where it belongs. But when they ask questions, it's your opportunity to address their concerns with a depth of knowledge and enthusiasm. This is where you use feature-and-benefit statements to sell your clients on your products and services.

Step Four: The trial close

Using trial closes throughout your sales presentation is a good idea because they provide valuable feedback every step of the way and let you know whether you and your clients are headed in the same direction. Examples of trial closes:

✔ So how does this feel to you?

✔ How do you like that feature?

✔ What do you think of the bathroom?

✔ You seemed to like the basement. Am I right about that?

✔ The kitchen seems to fit your lifestyle perfectly—doesn't it?

✔ Is this something that could work for you?

✔ Can you explain to me how this might work into your lifestyle?

✔ How does this address your concerns about travel time to and from work?

Step Five: Overcome objections

Objections can crop up at any point in the presentation. They are a natural part of the buying-and-selling process, and successful agents become good at interpreting them and resolving them in everyone's favor. The fact is that some objections are real and others are smoke screens designed to stall, overcome fear, gain more information, or because of the simple need to think. Objections should not be viewed as negative but as a client's need for more information.

Objections should not be viewed as negative but as a client's need for more information.

Three steps for handling objections

1. Bounce the objection back to them so they know you heard it and that you are listening.

2. Ask a double-ended question to again single out the real objection.

3. Once you are sure you have the real objection, repeat it once again and address that objection so they know you understand what they are saying.

Here's a situation with a client who doesn't want to sign right away:

Agent: Now that we have discussed agency relationship and who is representing whom, authorizing this agreement will establish the basis for our working relationship. (Put the agreement in front of them.)

Client: We would prefer not to sign anything today.

Agent: I can appreciate your thinking that way about authorizing an agreement. Is your hesitation because I have not thoroughly explained the agency relationship, or is it a general distrust of the real estate community and how it works?

Client: No, it is not you; you did a great job of explaining it to us.

Agent: Then is it a trust factor with me?

Client: Well actually, it has nothing to do with you. We worked with an agent before, and they had us sign this and made the contract for one year and did not allow us to easily get out of it. We had a bad relationship and it was difficult to sever the relationship.

Agent: I can now understand how that kind of experience would affect you.

By asking a double-ended question, we get to the real objection.

(What we're talking about in this scenario is not terms of an agreement but an agent's beliefs about how to build a relationship with clients. If you're delivering excellent service to your customers, there's no need to lock them into lengthy agreements that do nothing to strengthen your relationship. If you need terms on the contract that keep clients locked in to you, you use those terms as a substitute for what clients actually value. Making a shorter agreement—for three months—gives you and your clients flexibility that you both need. If you're doing a great job, you can renew it. If not, the client has an out. Better yet, you can put on the agreement that it can be unilaterally, or one without the other, terminated with immediate written notice. Again, that gives you both some protection against a relationship that isn't serving your needs. Using non-threatening terminology such as "authorizing the agreement" instead of "signing the contract" gives the client an equal footing. Authorizing an agreement is less threatening than "signing a contract" and helps maintain a cooperative versus an adversarial tone in your relationship.)

Step Six: Create mental word pictures

One of the most effective ways to help someone take ownership of the working relationship is to create word pictures that help clients envision the benefits and feelings they will experience once they have taken action with you.

The following is a possible dialogue:

Agent: When we first sat down, you said you were frustrated with missing some of the houses you wanted because by the time you got to see them at the Open House on Sunday, they were already sold. We can make that stress-free by sending you an e-mail the minute the property goes on the market. That way, you can be one of the first parties through the home the day it comes on the market. With that kind of notification, you can casually view the property on your own with me and not have to deal with twenty others congregating around the house. Imagine how stress free and effective this home search process can be!"

Step Seven: Bring closure to the presentation and commitment to the relationship

One of the most common mistakes agents made is to provide clients with easy ways out of the deal. They ask closed-ended questions that enable clients to respond with a simple "yes' or "no."

Those answers can be fatal.

Two scenarios

You are at the end of your buyer presentation, and you want the client to authorize the buyer representation form.

Agent: "So do you want to sign this contract so we can get started?"

Client: "No."

Now you have to ask, "Why not?" and you have no idea what you're going to hear.

With an open-ended question, you get an answer you can work with.

Agent: So far throughout our discussion we seem to be on the same page. For us to get started working together, we simply need to authorize this agreement. Would you feel better setting it up on a three-month time frame or six-month duration?

This phrasing makes it a lot harder for clients to say "no," and if they say they still are not sure what they want to do, simply ask, "So what kind of arrangement would work best for you?" Most importantly, you're gaining information you can use as you progress through the sales presentation.

In summary, this six-step selling process can single-handedly take you from closing five out of ten presentations to nine out of ten. The better your closing ratio, the less prospecting you have to do to make your goals—and the less expensive each sale becomes.

Use this worksheet to form your own SELLING PROCESS statements and dialogue that is your style.

Agent: _____

_____

Client: _____

_____

Agent: _____

_____

Client: _____

_____

Agent: _____

_____

Client: _____

_____

Agent: _____

_____

Client: _____

_____

Agent: _____

_____

Client: _____

_____

Agent: _____

_____

Offensive versus Defensive Selling

Another tactic is to use offensive versus defensive selling. True selling is in part the process of attaining clients. The activities you do and time you take to acquire them is called offensive selling. The more clients, the more relationships, and the more sales.

You can turn defensive selling (providing existing customers with valuable service) into offensive selling (acquiring new referred customers).

Once you have clients, anything you do to service and maintain them is called defensive selling because you are not working to obtain them—they are already your customers and you now are simply working to provide them with memorable service.

However, if you want to build a referral-based business and get referrals from the clients you have, you can turn defensive selling (providing existing customers with valuable service) into offensive selling (acquiring new referred customers). You do that by making the time you spend with existing clients as valuable for them as possible. For example, you can turn a simple walk through a house into an opportunity to train, educate, and empower buyers with knowledge about how to purchase a home. Educate them on grading, roof ages, mechanical operations and condition, and construction quality and methodology. When you do that, you are creating an impression that they are likely to share with family and friends.

The education you provide is part of the value you add to the transaction. Value that gets added in the process of providing a service can be hard to recognize, but the coffee business provides a good illustration of how value is added through a series of steps in the sales process. A coffee bean grower sells a bean to a distributor for a penny. The distributor adds value by making the bean available to coffee shops and sells that coffee bean to the coffee shop for a dime. The coffee shop grinds it up, adds hot water and a little chocolate, and makes it available at a convenient, comfortable location, and sells it to the consumer for $4.65. The value added in the process includes how little time the consumer has to spend to obtain the drink (doesn't have to travel to Colombia for the coffee; doesn't have to have a cup to put it in; doesn't have to milk a cow to get the cream; doesn't have to build the espresso machine, and has a warm, comfortable atmosphere in which to enjoy the drink).

My first year out of college, I worked for an outstanding *Fortune* 500 foodservice provider that supplied to restaurants, schools, and hospitals. I had to walk into the back of a chef's kitchen in a fancy restaurant where they were buying whole turkeys for $0.69 cents a pound. My job was to sell them on the idea of spending $4.69 cents a pound for a skin-on, in-the-bag, boneless, set-in-the-oven, tender turkey breast. It was scary, but I was successful the majority of the time. Why? The sales force was trained in selling value-addedness. I would determine the average hourly wage, the average amount of waste using a whole turkey, the inconsistency of flavor and texture doing it that way, and the time spent cleaning up. When I added up all those costs and showed my customers the real price per pound of what they were buying, they were well in favor of our patented product.

Value-addedness is not the price someone pays for something. It is the value one gets out of the product or service that is always based in part on the quality of the experience your customers have while working with you.

Value-addedness is always based in part on the quality of the experience your customers have while working with you.

Another important step is to follow-up. Again, what you do before and after the sale is as important as what you do during the presentation.

After the meeting, always be sure to send out a "Thank You" with a personalized note.

Call clients back to be sure they are comfortable with what took place, and reaffirm your desire and ability to serve their wants and needs as discussed in the meeting.

The follow-up material you send will help solidify their desire to work with you. It is all the little things that are easy to do that make the difference between **building a quality relationship** versus **doing a transaction.**

Pre-appointment activities

✔ Thank you to referral source

✔ Thank you to potential client

✔ Ask the referral source for any helpful information

✔ Tell the referral source how you will handle the transaction/relationship

✔ What time frame are they thinking about

✔ Where are they at in the process

✔ What time is a good time for the meeting

✔ What is the length of time they can devote to the meeting

✔ Send them to web site

✔ Listing packet/buyer packet

Post-appointment activities

✔ Thank you

✔ Letter confirming the points of the meeting so they know you were paying attention and taking notes

✔ Let referral source know how it went

✔ Provide any answers or information they had requested

✔ Having a compelling argument statement or message

Glossary of Terms

Benefit. The gain one receives from the feature of the product/service.

Closed-ended question. A question resulting in either a "yes" or "no" answer.

Feature. The tangible, physical characteristics of something.

Gaining commitment. Asking for the order.

Mental word picture. Having the client imagine how they would feel if they already owned the product/service.

Open-ended question. A question that requires the individual to answer with a sentence/paragraph response.

Sales objection. Most often thought of as a hurdle or no to a request for commitment, instead is indicating that there is still a question in that person's mind left unanswered.

Script. Predetermined set of words used to perform a conversation.

Selling Process. A methodical process and approach to helping the client get to the desired end result of a sale.

Trial close. Asking a question to gain commitment to a sale.

The Selling Process

1. Building rapport and establishing common ground

✔ Big picture open-ended question to determine what clients wants

✔ Confirm answer

✔ Bring down red flags

2. Determine wants, needs, and why

✔ Ask permission to ask questions

✔ Ask questions about how you can be of service

3. Establish belief and trust

✔ Feature/benefit selling statements

✔ Address the questions asked in determining their needs and wants

4. Trial close

✔ Ask for a commitment

✔ Open-ended question

5. Overcoming objections

✔ Restate the objection

✔ Agree with their concern being valid

✔ Ask a question with a potential real and not real answer to determine if true objection

6. Creating mental word pictures

✔ Ask them to "imagine"

✔ Take all the things they said they needed, confirm they are correct, and ask them to think how things would be thinking forward to already being in that result

7. Gaining commitment

✔ Ask them for an open-ended "alternative" answer for commitment

✔ Assume the sale with a tone of confidence in your voice and demeanor (as a matter of fact-ness)

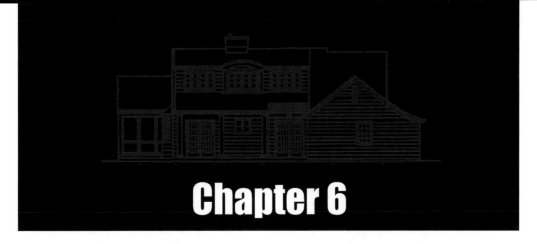

Chapter 6

It's Marketing Value and a Trusted Brand

*"I don't know the key to success but the key to failure is
trying to please everybody."*

—Bill Cosby

The purpose of marketing is to put yourself in front of a customer at the right time, at the right place, with the right product at the right price—with the right message. It's not hard to come up with dozens of ways to market yourself: direct-mail postcards, newsletters, flyers, brochures, websites, logos, stationery and business cards, coupons, buck slips, premiums, and more. At any given time any of them can work or fall flat. But it's not the vehicle that matters as much as its content and the style in which you present it, and when it comes to being a real estate agent, the content and style have to convey one idea if you want to succeed in this business: the value you bring to the buying or selling transaction.

This is an acute problem for agents because of the intangible nature of the services we provide. A product is a tangible object whose value can be assessed in terms of the raw materials that go into it plus the time and labor it takes to produce it. Products have tangible features and benefits (things you can touch, feel, smell, and see):

Ball Point Pen

Feature	Benefit
Thin	easy to hold
Rubber finger grip	non slip, easier to write with
Retractable point	when not in use will not get you full of ink
Inexpensive	disposable and easy to afford

The actual costs of manufacturing each element of a pen can be measured in parts and labor and an exchange value. I pay you money, you hand me a pen, and we have exchanged two mediums of value: an object and money.

A service involves a less tangible exchange derived from that service felt through thoughts and feelings, and gratification from it is typically delayed. For example, a business is struggling to make a go of it. An accountant comes in and spends an hour with the owner of the company and says, "If you cut costs and increase sales, you will turn things around and start being successful—and here's how to do it."

The accountant leaves, the business owner implements the accountant's advice, and months later the business is off and running successfully. The bill from the accountant comes to the business owner and their immediate reaction is, "What, $240 per hour to sit and chat with me?!"

A service involves a less tangible exchange derived from that service felt through thoughts and feelings, and gratification from it is typically delayed.

In reality, if the accountant had not provided the hour of advice, the business owner would still be struggling, but the value of the accountant's advice and how it helped the business owner improve the bottom line is intangible and difficult to measure. Knowledge, experience, and wisdom are all difficult to put a direct value on. That's why it's so important for agents to convey the value of the services they provide.

One example of a truly valuable service experience is Disney. They sell candy, rides, and entertainment—products—but they promote the experience, the memories, and the magic of having been there. In the words of Visa, the *experience* is priceless.

Agents sell the value of the services they provide by helping clients imagine the future in word pictures. "I'm going to give you a private showing of the properties on the market instead of having you compete with others in Open Houses!" Here you spell out the value of your personalized service by stressing the advantage of a private showing. The more you focus on the services you provide and the value they deliver in terms of features, advantages, and benefits, the more value clients perceive in you.

Clients have to take a leap of faith in you. Providing them with references will make that leap less frightening. And if you have painted word pictures in the minds of former clients, they will have words for describing the value of the services you provide when they talk to new prospects. If Disney is selling memories, you are selling a comforting experience that provides peace of mind; you provide guidance, experience, and expertise that take the guesswork out of the real estate transaction. Using statistics and your historical knowledge has the same effect. While building trust, you are also selling stress relief.

You are also selling yourself.

Brand has also grown to stand for a consistent set of values and impressions associated with you as a person and a company.

As a real estate agent, you are a key part of the product and the service represented by your brand. Branding in the old days was the process of putting your name on livestock to let ranchers know whose cows were whose. The basic act of branding is still to put your name on products and services so customers know they're yours. But the idea of a brand has also grown to stand for a consistent set of values and impressions associated with you as a person and a company.

The four Ps of marketing help you remember where to focus your attention when it comes to defining yourself and your brand.

Product. The services you provide, the features of the homes you represent, and the value of your expertise and professional experience.

Price. The combined cost and perceived value of what you sell and what you do for your customers.

Some of My 2004 Home Sales . . .

RICHMONDHILLSNEWS.COM

Place. Where you work, where your properties are, where you are willing to go for your customers, where your customers are.

Promotion. What you say about yourself and your properties —how, why, where, when and to whom you say it.

When the four Ps work together, they present a coherent, consistent image to your customers. The challenge of the four Ps is to ensure that each interaction with customers fosters the same perceptions about you and your company. That means words and imagery in your brochures, business cards, fliers, and website must work together to create a single consistent impression about what you and your business stand for. Because branding is so powerful in helping customers distinguish one agent from another, agents work hard to create unique brands for themselves through logos, tag lines, color palettes, and imagery.

Much of the brand you establish is determined by the market you are trying to reach.

Much of the brand you establish is determined by the market you are trying to reach. For example, if you are working with an executive-level client, you will probably present a sophisticated, professional look in all your materials. If your target is first-time home buyers, you may design your materials with a more fun, approachable, easy-going style. Regardless of which direction you take, product, pricing, place, and promotion that are consistent will send a clear message to customers and prospects about who you are and what you stand for.

If you claim to be a professional agent who only works with the best properties, a flimsy black-and-white brochure on see-through white

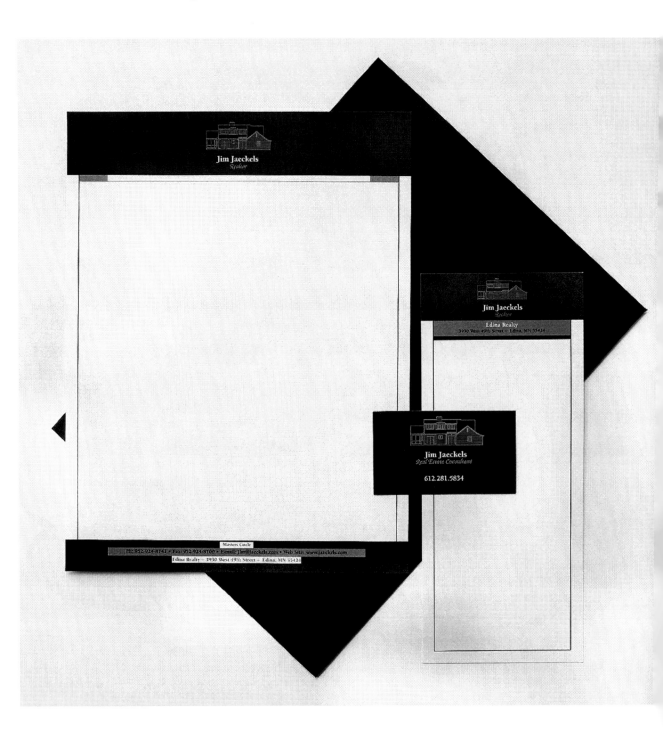

paper sends a contradictory message about who you are. Similarly, producing a heavy weight, four-color printed, double-sided glossy booklet of properties for a budget-minded clientele sends a confusing message about who you are and who you think your customers are.

The most important feature of a brand is its integrity. Establish a brand that is true to your skills, your mission, your knowledge, and your own best practices.

Another dimension of your brand is your marketing philosophy. One philosophy is to hire a team to execute a mass-market plan and to set goals for market share and a high-volume business. This book does not take a high-volume approach. Rather it spells out how to provide one-on-one service with clients so that when they hire *you* for *your* talents and abilities, they actually get you. By incorporating the information in this book you will become known as a "relationship-oriented real estate agent" versus a "transactional agent."

Being a relationship-oriented agent requires that you target specific market segments carefully. Since you are not taking a scattershot approach via mass mailings, you must identify segments by specific demographics such as age or income. Some agents specialize in clients who are recent empty nesters; others focus on clients of retirement age. Others set out to work primarily with professionals who must relocate due to demands of their careers. Still others focus on first-time home buyers or real estate investors or demographic variables.

In short, marketing is about knowing who you are and knowing who your customers are. When your marketing messages, presentations, and professional performance reflect that knowledge, you gain the trust of clients.

Chapter 7

It's Frequent, Thoughtful, Professional Written Communication

---

"It is not always what you say but how you say it."

—Anonymous

The letters in this chapter are designed to give you several ideas for giving customers the information they need for a successful real estate transaction. Sending letters remains one of the most effective ways of maintaining a strong relationship with clients, prospects, and business partners. They're effective because they're personal. When you send letters you're letting readers know that you're spending your time working for them.

Sincerity is the key to a good letter. Use your own voice. Use letters to share information, ask for referrals, provide buying and selling tips, or just to touch base and check in. When you take the initiative to stay in touch, people know you mean it when you say you want to do a great job for them.

There are lots of reasons to write letters. The ones in this chapter focus on providing value. There's no point in writing if you're not giving readers good reasons to read. So as you look through these letters, consider what kinds of value you can share with your customers.

2004 Thank You Super Real Estate Agent

In November's issues of *Twin Cities Monthly* and *Minneapolis St. Paul Magazine*, there was the Second Annual Publication of the "Super Real Estate Agents 2004."

The agents named represent 762 of the approximately 29,000 agents in Minnesota.

The periodicals surveyed recent homebuyers and sellers, mortgage and title companies, and the publication's subscribers to find the Top Agents in and near the Twin Cities.

Each respondent was asked to nominate real estate agents who they knew through personal experience and to assess them according to criteria that included integrity, market knowledge, marketing ability, communications skills, closing preparation, and overall satisfaction.

I am very fortunate to have been nominated for a second consecutive year.

My pledge on my website combined with my passion to be the best I can be at serving my clients and business associates is most rewarded by being appreciated by those I serve.

Having been nominated these two years is the ultimate compliment, and I am grateful to those of you who took the time and effort to respond to the survey.

"Jim's mission as a professional real estate agent is to provide you with superior representation services. A successful client relationship and your complete satisfaction are how Jim measures his success. He is positioned to maximize your value from any residential real estate transaction."

Dear Consummation to Closing

Congratulations on finding your new home. The purchase agreement is just the beginning of what follows to make sure everything from this point to closing goes smoothly. Attached please find the enclosure that helps to assure you have a problem-free move.

The following steps are an inspection (if elected), an appraisal, and title work. You will be involved in the inspection by setting it up and attending it (allow 2–3 hours). The appraisal and title work are done behind the scenes for you, but you will get the results from them.

You will then need to bring the following items to closing: paid receipt insurance binder, last ten years of residency, photo identification (driver's license), social security number, a cashier's check made to yourself, and an extra personal check for any possible extra expenses above and beyond the cashier's check if necessary. You usually get money back as lenders try to overestimate.

Though I will orchestrate this all, you will be having a lot of direct contact with the above entities. Contact me if you are having any problems.

It is not unusual for some "hick-ups" to occur during this time period from consummation to closing, but with constant contact and follow-through, all should go extremely well.

Sincerely,

Dear New Client

Thank you for deciding to work with me as your real estate agent to represent and assist you in your search for a new home.

My goal is to make this a fun and exciting experience for you, to help you get the most house for the least money, and to find a house that is both comfortably affordable for you and is a good investment.

I want you to take ownership of your home search as well so you can be educated on the process. The knowledge you gain will benefit you in this unusually dynamic marketplace where at present there are more buyers than sellers.

My pledge is to give you the utmost in service, care, and consideration—from the initial meeting through long after you start living in your new home. I want to be your "Real Estate Agent for Life."

As we search for your property, please be patient and know that there are a lot of people looking for a finite number of properties and there could be some ups and downs. My goal is to minimize those for you.

Thanks again for working with me. I will value and enjoy the opportunity to serve you!

Sincerely,

Dear Potential Home Buyer/Seller

As changes in your life take place, so perhaps does the need for new housing arrangements.

As a real estate agent, I work with all sorts of clients but pride myself on working with first-time home buyers and people moving up into their second home. It is a special niche market that requires special skills and talents from an agent.

My goal is to make the home buying experience fun and exciting for you as I carry the burden of all the potential complexities. I want to assure you the following:

1) You get the best home value (most home for least amount of money)

2) You buy what you can "comfortably" afford; live within your financial means

3) You avoid buying a "money pit" and buy a home that will appreciate as an investment to help you build equity and a nest egg.

You can benefit from my experience by either attending one of my "Buyer's Seminars" or by meeting with me for a no obligation one-on-one 45-minute presentation.

I truly enjoy the happiness and excitement experienced by first-time buyers and folks moving up.

If you would be interested in either a buyer presentation or buyer seminar, please feel free to leave me a message at 924-8741!

Sincerely,

P.S. At the "Home Buyer Seminars" there will be a loan officer and inspection/appraisal professional attending to answer questions and ensure that you purchase a sound home for a solid investment.

Dear Potential Listing

Greetings! Per our conversation, please find some marketing materials along with this letter. Thank you for considering me as a potential candidate to represent you with your real estate transactions.

I would value and enjoy the opportunity to explore with you your options as you consider whether to make a move.

To make our time together more productive, please consider the questions below as you prepare for your meeting.

1)   What you think you could sell your home for?

2) What you like/dislike about your present home; what you are looking for in your potential future home, and why you want these things?

3) What do you feel needs to be done to prepare your home for sale should you sell?

4) What is your time frame so you can coordinate the transition in a way to minimize inconvenience?

5) Do you want the sale to be contingent upon the sale of your home?

6) Children's schooling itinerary.

7) For your proposed new home consider the following: location, price range, # bedrooms/bathrooms, style of home, # of garages, fireplace or not, proximity to area, square footage requirements, age of home and the like.

8) What qualifications, services, and characteristics you are looking for in the real estate agent you may hire?

9) Any additional questions, concerns, thoughts, or feelings you may have as you consider the potential proposition.

I look forward to meeting you and your children Tuesday evening.

Sincerely,

Listing letter

As we approach the new millennium, real estate and all that comes with it is not immune to the challenges and demands of this new era.

The days of putting a sign in the front yard and hoping the house sells are obsolete. Or riding around in a car with a buyer a few times and then sitting at a closing table. And with that, so should be many of the ways of conducting traditional real estate transactions and representation.

So how will working with me be different from the other 8,000 choices in the Twin Cities? My commitment to you is that I will assure you that you will receive the utmost in professional real estate representation. You are not a transaction, but a long-term business and personal relationship.

My beliefs, skills, and philosophies go far beyond the traditional ways of handling real estate. What I bring to the table for you, first and foremost, is real estate experience and knowledge. But that is where it can end for most. You can expect full-service representation from the minute you contact me to years beyond your closing date. This brings a whole new meaning to the phrase, "Full-service Real Estate Agent for Life."

You will not just sell or buy a home with me. Rather, I will manage the entire process and offer services and experience in areas far beyond that. More importantly, you can depend on me to listen intently to your cares, concerns, and motivations whether you are buying, selling, or transitioning. And I will deliver results always cognizant of fulfilling expectations with effective communication.

I would both value and enjoy the opportunity to represent you in your real estate transactions and would spare absolutely no expense of time, energy, or financial resources to assure, to the best of my ability, your total satisfaction.

Sincerely,

Dear client holiday season letter

As the holiday season once again is upon us, I want to take this opportunity to provide you with a printout of the sold properties in your area, an update on the Twin Cities real estate market, my gratitude to those responsible for me earning the Twin Cities Real Estate SuperAgent award, a request from you to help me grow my business, a wish to all of you for the upcoming holiday season and New Year.

The enclosed "solds" in your area can help you get a feel for what your home may be worth. Knowing its value can help you determine equity should you think about moving, allow you to rid yourself of "Private Mortgage Insurance," and provide you with how much money may be available for a home equity loan. What is important to take from the printout is the average "price/square foot," not average price.

The Twin Cities to date is having its third best year in history, keeping in mind that the previous two have been unprecedented. The challenge is that housing inventory has increased from 16,000 properties two years ago to 70,000 today. When it was a seller's market, there was one home for every five buyers. Now, conversely, there are seven homes for every one buyer.

So what does that mean?

Buyers are discriminating, patient, unwilling to compromise, wanting "like-new" condition, and wanting to feel like they "got a deal." It is an opportunistic time for buyers to purchase homes.

So as sellers, simply put, one has to have a) good location, b) minimal knock-out factors, c) as close to perfect condition and staging as possible, d) appropriate pricing, and e) utilizes a full-service company and agent's marketing to gain the most exposure and product/service offerings as possible.

The other factors that affect salability are those things that cannot be controlled by the agent and seller such as interest rates, seasonality, competition, and domestic/world matters.

Thank you to those of you who were responsible for my achieving the 2006 Twin Cities Minneapolis/St. Paul Super Agent Award for the fourth straight year. This award is earned not on volume of business but instead from survey results indicating client, associate, lender, and title people's satisfaction with regard to the agent's abilities of negotiation, marketing, preparing the home for sale, proper pricing, finding the right home for the buyers, follow-through, and general customer service.

The real estate industry is undergoing a much overdue "cleansing" process whereby agents, lenders, title people, appraisers, and inspectors who jumped on the proverbial bandwagon are now being weeded out.

I look at this as an opportunity to continue to grow my business through referrals. As always, I want you to emphatically know that whether someone lives in Lino Lakes or Edina, is selling a $1,000,000 home or buying a $100,000 condominium, is your friend, family member, neighbor, or work associate, *I would both value and enjoy the opportunity to serve them.*

Feel assured that they would receive the utmost in representation services.

Sincerely,

Dear New Listing Client

The main reason for this letter is to express my whole-hearted appreciation to you for having the vote of confidence in me to market your property.

Feel assured that you will get an unequivocal effort of time and a well-financed marketing program dedicated to you and your property to net you the most amount of money with the least amount of inconvenience and market time.

Remember, like any relationship, communication is key to the success—spelling out the expectations up front and offering continuous, immediate, and openly mutual feedback to each other.

I truly see the value in your property and am excited to get going. Please refer to the enclosed calendar as a guideline for upcoming activities and retain the listing folder should any questions arise.

Finally, your best offers and most critical time for this property to sell are the first two to three weeks. Please read the listing information provided to you earlier to have a better understanding of what is in store based on industry history.

Thanks again and please contact me at the numbers on my business card should you have any questions.

Sincerely,

Dear New Listing

Just a quick note to say I truly appreciate the opportunity you have provided to me to represent you in the listing of your property.

Know that you and your property will receive the utmost in service, marketing, and a well-financed and comprehensive listing program.

Let's keep the communication open as it is critical to success and a positive working relationship.

Feel free to contact me at any of the numbers on my card.

Sincerely,

Dear Prepare for Sale Letter

First and foremost, thank you so much for the opportunity to help you with the selling of your home.

Please feel confident that you will receive the utmost in professionalism and service from me.

You have an absolutely wonderful home. Great karma which means there is a lot of "love" and family feeling when you walk into it. This is something no paint or staging can give a home. It either has it or it doesn't so kudos to you for that.

What follows is a list of "Home Highlights" I made note of on the property. Please add to it as you have lived there 21 years and I was there for about two hours.

Additionally, I have made a "To-do" list for you. Please, please understand that "a home that someone lives in" and "a home that someone is selling" are two different things. Therefore, please know that the following suggestions are to do the things that will appeal to the "general public" by de-personalizing the home, which is not always comfortable for the seller.

The key here is that we have constant two-way open communications.

Warmest Regards,

Dear Service Provider

The reason for this letter is to let you know that I would like the opportunity to make you and the other attached business professionals available to my clients and friends as a product/service resource.

You have been chosen as a result of my own personal experiences of satisfaction when having worked with you in the past for either myself or my clients and friends.

I want to thank you in advance for your professionalism and service mentality when working with future customers that I refer.

Likewise, if I can ever be of assistance to you or anyone you know needing assistance with a real estate matter, from buying and selling to renovating and restoring, please feel free to contact me.

Thanks, and have a great year and beyond!

Sincerely,

Comparative Market Analysis Letter

The reason for this letter is to keep you updated on the latest appreciation of your specific area.

On the whole, the Twin Cities has enjoyed an amazing "average" of 10–12% appreciation over the last two years.

Knowing your value can help you—

✔ Determine equity should you be thinking about moving

✔ Allow you to rid yourself of that monthly "Private Mortgage Insurance" premium you may be paying if you "haven't been" at 80%/20% loan to value

✔ Let you know how much money is available should you want a home equity loan.

IMPORTANT: You can receive a detailed e-mail of the enclosed properties, which would help you determine your equity for yourself, or I could always at no cost, no obligation, come out to do a comparative market analysis.

Your current e-mail address is presently not in my records, so if you want to e-mail me at my e-mail address and provide me with it, I can e-mail you the detailed properties and other useful home ownership information.

Take care, and keep in touch!

Sincerely,

Dear CMA Friends/Sphere

Happy New Year! Hopefully you had a great holiday season!

Over the holidays many friends and family members asked, "What do you think is going to happen with the crazy housing market?" and "Can you determine for me what my home is now worth?"

I do not have a crystal ball or claim to be able to predict the future, but reliable sources and continued research would lead me to believe that 2004 looks to be another great year for the Twin Cities real estate market, perhaps even enjoying the 10% plus appreciation we have enjoyed recently.

Interest rates are always subject to many uncontrollable variables, but if things hold true to form, they should stay at or near where they have been. I am not a licensed mortgage lender so cannot quote rates, but a range has been between four to seven percent depending on an adjustable rate mortgage or a fixed rate product.

To answer the "what is your home worth" question, an exact comparative market analysis would need to be conducted, free and with no obligation.

That having been said, I have enclosed some of the homes that sold last year in your area to give you a general idea of property values.

Hopefully you enjoy the information and let me know if I can answer any other questions.

Finally, because my business is strictly referral based, I would both value and enjoy the opportunity to assist you or anyone you know with your/their real estate needs.

As always, I value our friendship and look forward to seeing or talking with you some time!

Warmest Regards,

Dear Move

Congratulations! You're home at last! My wish for you is that this home brings all the peace, contentment, and enjoyment that a home should bring someone.

It has been a valuable and enjoyable experience for me to work with you, and I want you to know that I hope this is just the beginning of a long and lasting friendship and real estate working relationship. I want to be your "Real Estate Agent for Life!"

If there is anything I can do to improve my service to my clients, please let me know very candidly so I can work to be the best I can be in the industry.

If, on the other hand, I did a great job representing you in your home sale, I would appreciate your passing on the good word to others as I depend solely on referrals for my business and livelihood.

I will be contacting you to see how the move in and acclamation period went.

Bye for now and again…thanks and congratulations!

Dear Offer Recipient

On behalf of my friend and client, Judy Doe, we want to thank you for your consideration of her offer.

We hope that you find the terms and conditions of the offer suitable to you so that we can arrive at a win-win transaction.

Judy lived in the 50th and France area for years and having lived in Deephaven, desires to move back to an area that is comfortable and familiar to both her and her daughter, Susie.

The best means to reach me to facilitate information is on my cell phone at 952.555.1212

Thank you again, and Judy would enjoy consummating this transaction with you.

Sincerely,

Dear Referred Person

The reason for this letter is to simply introduce myself to you and provide you with some information should you or anyone you know ever be in need of real estate representation services.

I worked with Renee and Scott Johnson on their home search, and they were kind enough to pass on your name to me as someone I may be able to help some day.

You can feel confident that you will not be bombarded with phone calls or direct mail literature, but instead I will try to supply you with valuable, real estate-related information and keep my name in front of you in a tactful, professional way.

Please take some time to look at my web site as it is the best way to get an idea of my philosophies and qualifications.

I would both value and enjoy the opportunity to be of service to you!

Sincerely,

Dear Seller Consummation to Closing

Congratulations! I am extremely excited about your having decided to work with her on the sale of your home.

Enclosed please find information that will make for a smooth transition along with an idea of what is forthcoming and who is responsible for what activities.

Please know that I will be orchestrating everything, but there will be some things you will need to be involved with in the process as follows:

The closer is Mary Smith, 952.923.5858.

Enclosed please find:
- ✔ Seller's Net Sheet
- ✔ "Closing Process" Brochure
- ✔ Moving Guide
- ✔ Postal Moving Kit
- ✔ Request to provide Closer with Title Information (Abstract or Torrens)
- ✔ Request to provide Closer with Loan Payoff Information

We now have the inspection, appraisal, and walk-through for buyer the day before closing. . . . and closing.

Please feel free to contact me should you need anything at 612.555.2160.

Sincerely,

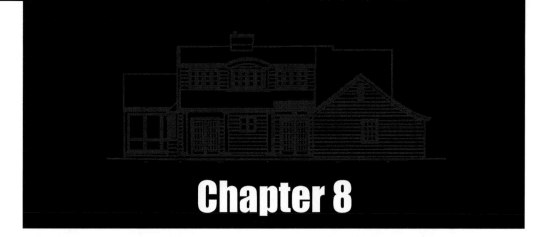

Chapter 8

It's a Presentation with Staying Power

"Buyers are liars."

—Industry known quote

The goal of this chapter is to improve your presentation skills because they are a key to earning, building, and maintaining buyer loyalty. Agents spend a considerable amount of time on sales presentations to buyers and sellers, one-on-one, during Open Houses, and throughout the day on the phone and via e-mail, so presentation skills are critically important to an agent's success. The goals of a sales presentation include more than making a sale. It's during presentations that you will drive home the key points about the four Ps and your brand of business.

An effective presentation will help customers think about what they are looking for in an ideal home. Use presentation time to gather information about the customer's preferences, to test features and benefits of listings on customers, and to sharpen your understanding of what an ideal home is for each customer. Many clients will be able to spell out what they are looking for, but many will not, and you will save yourself and your clients valuable time by clarifying what your customer means by terms like *traditional, homey, spacious, classical,* and *comfortable.*

During presentations, you are selling a product and a service, so prepare for your first meeting with information about yourself. If you have sent them to your personal website ahead of time, you might begin by asking about their impressions of the site.

Price is about much more than the seller's asking price for the home. In your sales presentations, you must help define for your customer the value of the property AND the value of the services you provide. Drive home that you will be spending time drafting agreements, researching answers to their questions, providing data on which to base important decisions, negotiating with other parties—all of which will build your value to your customer. Because of the perception that contracts are boilerplate forms that an administrative assistant can fill out online, and that agents are part of a back-slapping wine-swilling cabal of insiders conspiring to separate innocents from their hard-earned cash, it's critical that you point out evidence to the contrary at every turn. Define yourself in terms of the relationships you have, the information resources you can access in seconds, the strategic alliances with title companies, lawyers, financial institutions, remodelers, and other service providers—your broader network of colleagues—all of whom surround your customer with resources that make the transaction as rewarding as possible.

You will present at kitchen tables, in living rooms, in buyers' homes and sellers' homes, in your office, at community meetings, trade shows, in coffee shops, and on the phone. On the one hand, the place dimension of your presentation offers some of the best opportunities for controlling the environment. Your own office is ideal in many respects because your files are at hand, as are your computer, a fax machine, and a photocopier. If a customer is interviewing other agents, a meeting at your office may be more effective in establishing a professional relationship that they will find more difficult to break than a relationship that begins at a more informal venue like a coffee shop. When you're on your own turf, you may feel more comfortable asking about the status of their agent search than you would at the client's kitchen table, where the question may seem more invasive.

Wherever you meet for the first time, have the following items ready in a customized folder:

- ✔ Agency Relationship and Exclusive Right to Represent the Buyer forms (varies by state)
- ✔ An Equal Opportunity/Non-Discrimination pamphlet
- ✔ A Lead Based Paint Booklet where applicable
- ✔ A client profile sheet
- ✔ A booklet on the home buying process
- ✔ A professionally designed personal brochure

Client Profile

Name:	
Home Address:	
Work Address:	
Referral Source:	
Work Phone #'s:	
Home Phone #'s:	
Cell Phone #'s:	
Fax #'s:	
E-mail addresses:	
Hours & preferred method of communication:	
Lender Name & Phone #:	
Title Company Closer & Phone #:	
Areas:	

Property Type:	Price Range:
Bedrooms:	Bathrooms:
School District:	Year Built:
Square Footage:	Style:
Garage Stalls:	Fireplace:

Other Search Criteria:
Notes:

At the beginning of the meeting, take time to build trust, credibility, and a comfort level by keeping the conversation focused on the customer.

Include refrigerator business card magnets, sports team schedules, a customized calendar, a map book as their home-finding bible, customized notepads, and other promotional items that keep your name in front of them and can be passed on to others.

At the beginning of the meeting, take time to build trust, credibility, and a comfort level by keeping the conversation focused on the customer. Ask about their wants, needs, and desires and just as importantly, **why** they want what they want.

- ✔ So how do you feel about the adventure that lies ahead: nervous, excited, happy, concerned?
- ✔ Where are you in the process: are you just beginning, do you know what you're looking for, are you pre-qualified, do you need negotiation assistance?
- ✔ Have you met with a lender?
- ✔ What do you think of what you have seen on the market so far?
- ✔ What do you know about the home-buying process?
- ✔ Do you have any questions about me or my company before we begin?
- ✔ What are your expectations of your agent and the relationship?
- ✔ Is anyone else involved in the process so far?

You must let your customers know that it's their meeting, not yours. Demonstrating that you are sincerely interested in their needs and desires is critical in the first meeting.

Although it's your customer's meeting, it's appropriate and desirable to have an agenda. Providing guidance helps keep everyone on task and makes the best use of time. Having an agenda shows respect for everyone's time. Take time to explain your relationship with your agency and how the relationship benefits your customer.

Fill out the client profile, explaining that it is for gathering information that will be needed during the relationship and process. You need the following information:

- ✔ address, phone numbers, e-mail addresses
- ✔ best times to communicate
- ✔ who to contact, in order of priority
- ✔ how to communicate, i.e., phone versus e-mail
- ✔ home features and whether they are must haves, would-likes, or don't-matters
- ✔ geographic interests or constraints
- ✔ ideal minimum number of bedrooms, bathrooms, garage stalls
- ✔ ideal minimum square footage
- ✔ year built and style preference
- ✔ fireplace or not
- ✔ other features: fenced yard, larger living room due to accommodating a grand piano, being near transportation systems, schools, religious affiliations, and family.

Take notes during this discussion. It shows your interest and helps you keep track of the details.

Financial information can be handled in a number of ways depending on the agent, but the most relevant issues in the early stage of buying is the buyer's pre-approval:

Agent: Although we work closely together, I don't get involved in your personal finances. That is something between you and your lender. I do have to understand your comfort level with price ranges so we can work together to get you pre-approved for a mortgage through a reputable lender. I don't want to cause frustration by showing you homes you fall in love with only to find that they are not in your price range.

Discuss the client's lender, if your client has one, and investigate the lender's authenticity. If your client doesn't have one, offer references to your list of lenders. Even if your client has a lender, suggest getting a second opinion or even second pre-approval as it makes the client a stronger buyer in an offer presentation.

Investigate the lender's authenticity.

Buyers and sellers of real estate, along with the general population, prefer one-stop shopping or having all the related services under one roof for simplicity, a reduction in time and stress, and potential cost savings. Make it clear during your presentation that you promote the value of your customers' relationship with you by describing the value of your relationships with other service providers. That's how you become the one-stop-shop in your customers' eyes.

What else to learn during your presentations? Determine your clients' time frame for closing. Your clients may be tied into a lease, waiting for an inheritance, have to save for a down payment, or be free and clear and want to find something immediately. Understanding clients' timing issues tells you how serious they are and if you are working with ready, willing, and able buyers.

Explain time frames of the buying or selling process, how long it generally takes to find the right home, have it appraised and inspected, complete the title work and walk-through scheduled so they can back into the equation of when to begin.

Thoroughly explaining the home-buying process helps establish trust with clients. It's also a way of positioning yourself to show how you are different. For example, making the following points will distinguish you as an agent who puts the client first:

Agent: My experience has shown that agents typically will withhold information from the clients regarding the process because it creates a dependent relationship in which clients feel they cannot make a move without the agent. Some agents try to create dependency out of a sense of insecurity.

I, on the other hand, understand that you want and need information. You want to be knowledgeable and empowered along the way to pro-actively make decisions about the process—take ownership of it.

That's why I explain the steps of the process up front and counsel you so you can tell me what you want to do. This does not mean that you do all the work, but instead that I take the burden of the details and issues that ultimately arise and carry them on my shoulders so you can enjoy what should be a stress-free experience.

Explain how to use the multiple listing service (MLS) for the search process right at the start, so clients understand it. When you meet at your office, you can be sure that the MLS will be working and can orient clients to the online resources they can access by working with you. Type in their search criteria so they can see for themselves the search process, which may be the most exciting part of the meeting for them.

It is important to have the client in your car at least for the first time out.

When you leave the office to visit a property, it is important to have the client in **your** car at least for the first time out. This builds rapport and you get immediate input and feedback. This is where the client does the talking and you do the listening.

As you drive to the property, point out features of the surrounding community and homes: the value of the surroundings apply by association to the value of the property in question. Draw attention to parks, bikeways, restaurants, lakes, shopping, and other amenities of convenience.

Potential negative factors could be railroad tracks, power lines, commercial buildings, industrial areas, airplane noise, busy highways and streets, mixed zoning areas, and the general condition and architecture of the surrounding homes. You will want to point these out as well.

The approach, or drive up to the home, is important for a good first impression. Upon arriving at the home, present clients with a home checklist on the reverse side of the listing sheet to keep track of the homes they have seen and to rate items such as condition, yard, floor plan, neighborhood, style, changes to make, and pluses and minuses of each home so that they can remember what they have seen. The following is a possible dialogue:

Agent: This is what I have found is the best way to handle showings. You can walk through the home uninterrupted so you can take it all in. Homes are like people. They all have personalities of scent, structure, ambiance, and just a general feeling to them. You need to be able to focus on that.

Additionally, I won't make comments about taste-related things as they are all unique and personal, such as choices in wallpaper, carpeting, and kitchen cabinets. It is after all your home, not mine.

That having been said, as a matter of counsel affecting condition or value, I will walk you through the property inside and out and explain the positives and negatives I see. I will also point out, at least on the initial houses we look at as a matter of education for you, what to look for in a home, such as grading on the outside, exterior maintenance, downspout lengths, and roof conditions.

On the interior, the bones of the home, I will pay attention to the structural integrity of its foundation and the plumb of the house; the age and condition of the mechanicals like plumbing, electrical, heating and air conditioning, water heater, appliances, and water softener and filtration system—where applicable.

Ask for the buyer's assessment of the home; their likes and dislikes; maybe rate it on a scale from 1 to 10 or even rate it compared to others they have toured. After several showings or at a point when they show strong buying signals, have along a ***blank purchase agreement***. Use it to familiarize buyers with the form, so they feel empowered and knowledgeable about how to fill it out when the

PURCHASE AGREEMENT
This form approved by the Minnesota Association of REALTORS®,
which disclaims any liability arising out of use or misuse of this form.
© 2007 Minnesota Association of REALTORS®, Edina, MN

1. Date   March 7, 2008 _____

2. Page 1 of _____

3. RECEIVED OF _____

4. _____

5. the sum of _____ Dollars ($ _____)

6. by ☐ CHECK ☐ CASH ☐ NOTE as earnest money to be deposited upon acceptance of Purchase
    ------(Check one.)------

7. **Agreement by all parties, on or before the third business day after acceptance, in the trust account of listing**

8. **broker, unless otherwise agreed to in writing, but to be returned to Buyer if Purchase Agreement is not accepted**

9. **by Seller.** Said earnest money is part payment for the purchase of the property located at

10. Street Address: _____

11. City of _____ , County of _____ ,

12. State of Minnesota, legally described as _____

13. _____

14. _____ ,

15. including all fixtures on the following property, if any, owned by Seller and used and located on said property,

16. including but not limited to garden bulbs, plants, shrubs and trees; storm sash, storm doors, screens and awnings;

17. window shades, blinds, traverse and curtain and drapery rods; attached lighting fixtures and bulbs; plumbing

18. fixtures, water heater, heating plants (with any burners, non-fuel tanks, stokers and other equipment used in connection

19. therewith), built-in air-conditioning equipment, electronic air filter, water softener ☐ **OWNED** ☐ **RENTED** ☐ **NONE,**
    ------(Check one.)------

20. built-in humidifier and dehumidifier, liquid fuel tank(s) ☐ **OWNED** ☐ **RENTED** ☐ **NONE** and controls (if the
    ------(Check one.)------

21. property of Seller), sump pump; attached television antenna, cable TV jacks and wiring; **BUILT-INS:** dishwashers,

22. garbage disposals, trash compactors, ovens, cook-top stoves, microwave ovens, hood fans, intercoms;

23. **ATTACHED:** carpeting; mirrors; garage door openers and all controls; smoke detectors; fireplace screens, doors and

24. heatilators; **AND** the following personal property: _____

25. _____

26. _____

27. all of which property Seller has this day agreed to sell to Buyer for sum of ($ _____)

28. _____ Dollars,

29. which Buyer agrees to pay in the following manner:

30. 1. Cash of at least _____ percent (%) of the sale price, which includes the earnest money; PLUS

31. 2. Financing, the total amount secured against this property to fund this purchase, not to exceed _____

32. percent (%) of the sale price.

33. Such financing shall be (check one) ☐ **a first mortgage;** ☐ **a contract for deed;** or ☐ **a first mortgage with**

34. **subordinate financing,** as described in the attached *Addendum:*

35. ☐ *Conventional* ☐ *FHA* ☐ *DVA* ☐ *Assumption* ☐ *Contract for Deed* ☐ Other: _____ .
    ------(Check one.)------

36. The date of closing shall be _____ , 20 _____ .

37. This Purchase Agreement ☐ **IS** ☐ **IS NOT** subject to a *Contingency Addendum* for sale of Buyer's property.
    ------(Check one.)------

38. (If answer is **IS,** see attached *Addendum.*)

39. (If answer is **IS NOT,** the closing of Buyer's property, if any, may still affect Buyer's ability to obtain financing, if financing

40. is applicable.)

time comes. On a Sunday night in a multiple offer situation, you will not want to spend several hours going over a purchase agreement for the first time. Be prepared by going over the agreement in advance. Often an offer will be accepted based on the buyer being the first one prepared and sitting at the offer table.

Be prepared by going over the agreement in advance.

While you are viewing properties together, discuss the upcoming steps of the transaction, namely the inspection, appraisal, title work, walk-through, and closing. Taking this pro-active approach lets the buyer take ownership of the process, which builds trust with the agent and the industry in general.

Offer time! When it comes time to write an offer, it is best to do it at the office where there is access to computers, fax machines, copiers, and phones. Be on the computer together, and look at comparables to determine whether the property is priced right. If it is, discuss the seventeen variables that make an offer attractive.

If possible, write the offer on a "Forms-On-Line" for clarity, professionalism, and a state-of-the-art presentation. Walk through with the buyer the process of the presentation and negotiation: what happens to the earnest money, and what is an accepted, countered, or rejected offer. The details of the offer and how it is written up personal to each agent and are beyond the scope of this book. However, the offer should be written in a way to make the buyer as attractive to the seller with the right terms and conditions, yet in the best interest of the buyer and without foregoing basic home-buying principles. An example of making a buyer attractive is having them

PURCHASE AGREEMENT OFFER CONSIDERATIONS

- ☐ Financial worthiness of prospective buyer (pre-approved versus pre-qualified)
- ☐ Lender considerations
- ☐ Earnest money amount
- ☐ Offer price (net)
- ☐ Down payment and loan amount
- ☐ Closing date
- ☐ Type of financing
- ☐ Contingencies (sale of own residence, another purchase agreement, inspection)
- ☐ Assessment and taxes
- ☐ Possession time and date
- ☐ Representation
- ☐ Financing terms
- ☐ Inspection terms
- ☐ Personal property requests
- ☐ Additional requests
- ☐ Arbitration or litigation
- ☐ Anything else either tangible or intangible

"pre-approved" through one, maybe even two reputable, well-recognized lenders.

Write the offer on a "Forms-On-Line" for clarity, professionalism, and a state-of-the-art presentation.

Many in the industry rely heavily on technical means to conduct transactions, interacting almost exclusively via e-mail or fax. This is an injustice to all parties involved. Real estate agents are paid good money, and one of the most important parts of our job is to present an offer in person. When we communicate face-to-face—or at least over the phone—we offer more personal attention to detail than agents who don't. You represent the buyer more effectively by making opportunities to sell them to the listing agent and seller. Dialogue enables important questions or objections to be answered on the spot, and the selling agent can use salesmanship of eye contact, non-verbal communication, and voice inflections to build credibility and confidence with the listing agent and seller.

One should always have a pre-approval letter and a check in hand to go with the offer. Make a copy for the listing agent. Often listing agents will present the offer to their clients, and you can't count on controlling the presentation as the buyer's agent. Sometimes the best you can do is paraphrase the highlights of the offer for the listing agent to share with the seller.

Tell a bit about the buyers, why they chose to write on the seller's home, and complement the home and the listing agent for how things have been presented and handled. Typically, it is good to have the buyer in the office, should their signatures be needed to expedite the paperwork.

Paying special attention to detail at this stage will add value as emotions may be running high and clients are in more need of reassurance and peace of mind about the transaction. Arbitration and lawsuits are the least enjoyable parts of a real estate career and are easily avoided with just a little extra time up front.

Speaking of arbitration and lawsuits, it is the responsibility of the agent to keep abreast of all the legal and industry updates on everything from disclosure to updated forms. This is the only way you can possibly properly assist your client.

Keep abreast of all the legal and industry updates. This is the only way you can possibly properly assist your client.

My philosophy on negotiation of the offer is to do all the possible due diligence a layman can do with regard to the home's condition and value—and to be upfront about what you know. This knowledge must be reflected in the initial offer.

The purpose of the inspection is to adjust price terms and conditions based on anything that is hazardous or potentially expensive to the buyer and unforeseen at the time of making the initial offer. Some examples are a cracked heat-exchanger in a furnace, mold, or high radon gas levels.

There are different schools of thought on inspections. Some agents attend the entire inspection, some meet at the beginning or end, and others choose not to attend. This is once again a time to earn your keep, build rapport, and position yourself for future referrals. I suggest you meet the buyers at the inspection to do introductions and in some cases let the parties into the home. Then show up at the end only when the inspector is going through the property with the buyer. This allows buyers to feel that they are getting a candid, unbiased inspection, uncompromised by the agent's influence. A good inspector will be truthful, fair, and complete whether the agent is there or not.

Agents who attend the summary walk-through and see firsthand the potential issues with the home are in a better position to document and explain in detail to the listing agent and sellers any counter-offer requests or questions.

The appraisal process and title processes are pretty straight forward, but the key, once again, is being pro-active—keeping in touch with the people involved in the transaction. With the title, it is always a good idea to have the work turned over by the listing agent when the listing is first taken, so it can be worked on to avoid any last-minute surprises.

Agents have different philosophies for the walk-through process, too. Some think it is good to go the day of the walk-through, so you have every last chance to see the condition—before the sellers move out. Many think it is good to go the day before, so there is plenty of time to communicate problems or issues to be discussed without being in a last-minute time crunch to resolve them. Someone ends up compromising, and that leaves a bad taste in the mouth.

An agent can do 100 things right, but it seems the only thing the clients ever remember is what happens last. Hence the critical need for an outstanding closer/title person.

In any event, one thing to remind the buyers of prior to entering the home on the walk-through is that the home may seem different from when they had the initial offer accepted. Nail holes in the walls, carpet stains where furniture was or wasn't, no more good baked bread scent in the air.

Always, always attend the closing unless logistically impossible!

How you handle disputes is a matter of agent preference and one has to be guided by conscience and business philosophy. Disputes are common in any business, so how you handle them will have an effect on your reputation. If you don't return calls when there's a dispute, that fact may make its way into conversations your customers have with friends or colleagues. If you put a priority on dispute resolution, that too will be passed on to others.

Always, always attend the closing unless logistically impossible! You don't want clients thinking, "Oh great, my agent made the commission and has now disappeared." If you cannot make it, find someone to stand in for you.

The main reason for attending the closing is to handle problems that may arise, make sure that the buyer is comfortable and understands what is going on, and make sure the buyer's good faith and

U.S. Housing and Urban Development (HUD) statements are congruent. In addition, this is a good time to discuss the value of owner's optional title insurance and making sure that the buyer homesteads the property.

This is also a good time to provide closing gifts, ask for referrals, and explain how you will be in touch with them to make sure the move-in went well. Let them know that you will be in touch to provide information on home maintenance. Called value-added home ownership information, it is another way to be your customers' full-service real estate resource for life. Newsletters are a good medium for this.

Buyer Checklist

- ☐ Initial meeting
- ☐ Welcome letter and thank you
- ☐ Thank you to referral source
- ☐ Client profile
- ☐ Client profile confirmation letter/e-mail
- ☐ Initial search
- ☐ Offer
- ☐ Inspection
- ☐ Turn in file
- ☐ Fax lender
- ☐ Copy client
- ☐ Original in file
- ☐ Moving kit and letter
- ☐ Appraisal call
- ☐ Prepare for closing call
- ☐ Walk-through
- ☐ Thank you, referral letter
- ☐ Closing gift
- ☐ Closing
- ☐ Follow-up call

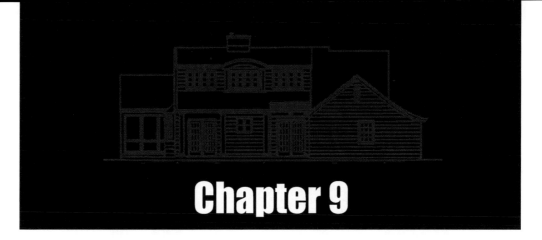

Chapter 9

In a Seller's Market or Buyer's Market, It's a Value Additude

"If you would convince others, be open to conviction yourself."

Depending on the market, working with sellers can be a simple process or a challenging one. If the home sells right away at the seller's asking price, terms, and conditions, the relationship can provide immediate satisfaction for everyone involved. When it is a seller's market, it feels like you can do no wrong: you simply put out a sign and the property is sold. When, on the other hand, it does not sell and is on the market a long time, working with sellers can be stressful.

In a buyer's market with lengthy market time, the situation calls for more of a project management process. You can maintain a great relationship with your client and actually use it as an opportunity to separate yourself from your competition by getting it sold when others cannot.

But the first thing you have to decide is whether you even want the listing. Sometimes "no thank you" can be the three best words in your sales strategy. If after meeting with the client you decide that the property is not sellable or that the seller has unrealistic expectations, a "no" is a perfectly sound response to the situation. One of the most important lessons agents have to learn is that clients who are unrealistic, demanding, and essentially wanting everything for nothing up front will be that way throughout the relationship. The harder you try to please them, the worse they get. When you have such a prospect, the best move is to refer the business to someone else and use your time in a more rewarding and productive way.

Clients who are unrealistic, demanding, and essentially wanting everything for nothing up front will be that way throughout the relationship.

If you do choose to work with the seller, you will spend a major portion of your time securing the listing. This process can take several forms and may include multiple strategies. Some agents like to use a one-step meeting process, while others prefer two and even three meetings to present their case in trying to secure the listing.

If you do your homework and incorporate a selling process into your presentation, it becomes a one-stop process. The best way to prepare for your first face-to-face meeting is to prepare questions that help you get at the value of the property and the primary concerns your prospects have about the selling process. Some questions are general; others are more targeted.

✔ How can I be of service to you?

✔ Why are you moving?

✔ What is your time frame for selling?

✔ How long have you lived in your present home?

✔ How are you feeling about the move?

✔ When did you purchase your home, and was it on the real estate agent network?

✔ What improvements have you made to your home—especially in terms of additional square footage?

If your prospect's home has never been on the market or the multiple listing service before to determine the property's characteristics, find the information necessary to do a preliminary market analysis, such as number of bedrooms, bathrooms, garage stalls, square footage, year built, and style. It is preliminary because you still have to see the property firsthand and know the condition of the home to determine a reasonable price.

If you are not sure whether a prospect is interviewing other agents, do not ask, "Are you interviewing any other agents?" because that will only plant the seed. Instead ask open-ended questions to find out. For example, "How are you going about the process of selling your home?" may lead to a response about the prospect meeting with several agents to find the right fit. Don't ask Yes/No questions because answers to such questions provide you with very little information. "Is the selling process going well for you?" may get you a "yes" or a "no" and not much else unless you ask follow-up questions. Why not get to those more important questions right off the bat? "What are some of concerns you have about selling your home?" is a question that gets at problems for which you will have solutions. That's also the kind of question that helps you build a stronger rapport with your prospect.

Asking prospects about their sales time frame tells you whether or not they have allowed adequate time for the selling process. If they haven't, you can give them more reasonable expectations.

The Appointment

Set the appointment for a time when you will have their undivided attention. Often this means when the children are napping or are in school. Out of respect for the seller's schedule, ask how much time they can devote to the meeting. Knowing that helps you plan your presentation, too.

Set the appointment for a time when you will have their undivided attention.

Typically the kitchen or dining room table is the best place to meet during your first visit as it is where people seem to be most comfortable. It is also a good spot to set out the information you will be going over. Asking sellers where they want to meet is a good idea, too—as a matter of courtesy and to maximize the seller's comfort.

If the seller asks if you want to tour the home, take advantage of the offer. It is a good idea for several reasons: a) the seller is obviously proud of their home and to say "no" could be interpreted to mean you aren't as interested in it as they want you to be, b) it gives you a chance to build rapport while walking around, which is more natural than sitting at the table, and c) it lets you determine the condition of the property, which can help you decide whether you want to represent the property and whether the asking price is appropriate.

Once you are seated with them, here is an example of how a presentation might go:

Agent: Thank you for having me out to your home. I would like to determine what your goal is for the meeting and what your questions, concerns, thoughts and feelings are about the process and our relationship. How does that sound?

Client: Sounds fine.

Agent: And by the time we conclude the meeting, you should be feeling comfortable that these things have been addressed. I want you to be confident that I am the right person to sell your home for you. There should be a mutual feeling of chemistry, as we will be spending a lot of time together, and the desire to work with each other is essential from the start. So let's get started. How about if you tell me what you are thinking.

Client: I'm thinking I don't know where to start.

Address the client's response then by letting them know that is why you are there—to help them get started, answer all their questions, and explain in detail how the whole program works. That is how you get in step with them mentally and let them know you are on the same team.

Typically, clients don't know what they don't know, so it's good to start with these most frequently asked questions.

What should be done to prepare the home for sale?

Help them by walking together through the home, room by room, making a to-do list for preparing the home for sale.

Your job is to help them make the home as appealing as possible at a cost that makes sense given the home, comps, and the market.

Explain what your company and you will do to market and sell the home for the most money and least amount of market time and inconvenience to the seller.

Spell out as simply as possible the steps you will take to sell the home, where you will list it, the Web tools you use, how many people you will reach with listings, when you will show the home, and other details of your sales and marketing plan. Features and benefits in my marketing strategy include—

- ✔ The Transaction Tracker System, which enables agents to follow and understand at all times what is going on with listings at the click of a mouse.

- ✔ Intra-office networking, which is how we get exposure for the property before it even hits the market through real estate agents networking verbally and by intra-office communication.

- ✔ A marketing campaign. We implement the most comprehensive and well-financed marketing campaigns in the industry. This is a pro-active approach versus reactive approach to attracting buyers to the home, thus achieving the greatest exposure, selling price, and net dollars with the least inconvenience.

Describe your marketing process so sellers understand what you do for them. "By implementing what I call my stacked marketing campaign, you get the most amount of exposure up front which is critical, but you also receive on-going, continuous process of marketing your property."

Explain how you will price their home: "A comparative market analysis will help you understand your marketplace so you can arrive at the price that will get you the highest return."

Notice in the statements above focus on "you" versus "I/me" to highlight benefits to the client and answer with conviction the questions the seller has about entering into the relationship.

The agent's commission rate is not the factor that influences the seller's income from the sale.

What is the home worth, and how much will they net out of the sale?

You have to address the commission question. It's natural for sellers to look for the lowest commission rate because they feel it saves them the most amount of money. This is ill-conceived thinking, however, because the agent's commission rate is not the factor that influences the seller's income from the sale. Help the seller focus on the "net amount" that they will take from the transaction instead.

For example, compare the two scenarios:

Seller One
- ✔ $200,000 sale price from discounted commission rate and limited marketing campaign
- ✔ $10,000 5% transaction fee
- ✔ $190,000 net to seller

Let's Estimate Your Net Proceeds*

1   Selling Price . . . . $_____ $_____

2   Present Mortgage . . . . $_____ $_____

3   Interest Adjustment (1-month/2-month if FHA) . . . . $_____ $_____

4   Pay Off of C/D, second Mortgage, Home Improvement Loan,
    Appliance Financing, etc.. . . . . $_____ $_____

5   Interest Adjustment (C/D, second Mortgage, etc., - one month) . . . . . . $_____ $_____

6   Pre-Payment Penalty on Mortgage . . . . $_____ $_____

7   Contract for Deed Discount _____% of $_____ . . . $_____ $_____

8   Special Assessments Levied, Certified . . . . $_____ $_____

9   Special Assessments, Pending
    (200% x estimated assessments to be escrowed) . . . . $_____ $_____

10 The amount on lines 8 and 9 are based upon figures obtained on
    _____ (date) from _____ . . . . . . $_____ $_____

11 Plumbers and Municipality Connection Fee (Sewer, Water) . . . . $_____ $_____

12 Brokerage Commission . . . . $_____ $_____

13 Brokers Administrative Commission . . . . $_____ $_____

14 Settlement Fee ($315 - Minn., $285 - Wisc.) . . . . $_____ $_____

15 Deed Tax (Minn. only $3.30/thousand) . . . . $_____ $_____

16 Abstract ($360-$460); RPA Fees ($200-$250)
    Title Insurance Commitment Cost ($370-$540) . . . . $_____ $_____

17 Special Assessment Search Fee ($35) Per PID . . . . $_____ $_____

18 Recording and Services second second Analysis Fees (Minn. $75-$250;
    Wisc. $25-$100) . . . . _____ $_____

19 Balance of Real Estate Taxes Due at Closing
    (Per Purchase Agreement) . . . . $_____ $_____

20 Discount Points ____% of $_____ of Buyer's New Mortgage . $_____ $_____

21 Seller's Paying Buyer's Closing Costs (Whatever Applies) . . . . $_____ $_____

22 DVA Funding Fee (Per Purchase Agreement) . . . . $_____ $_____

23 DVA Closing Fee, Tax Service Fee and Misc.
    Buyer Financing Fees on DVA Loans (approx. $390) (Buyer Cannot Pay) $_____ $_____

24 Misc. Buyer Financing Fees Charged to Seller on FHA Loans (approx. $165). $_____ $_____

25 Other Expenses: (Survey, Water Test, Soil Test, Insurance,
    Sealing Inoperable Well, Final Inspection Fees etc.) . . . . $_____ $_____

26 Association Re-Sale Disclosure Certificate ($25-$200) . . . . $_____ $_____

27 Balance of Association Dues Due at Closing (Per Purchase Aggreement) $_____ $_____

28 Dues Current Letter . . . . $_____ $_____

29 Local Building Inspection, if Required by Municipality:
    (Truth in Housing Report, etc.) . . . . $_____ $_____

30 Deed Preparation Fee (where applicable) . . . . $_____ $_____

31 Document Handling Fee ($25-$50) . . . . $_____ $_____

32 Total Estimated Selling Expenses (Lines 2 to 32) . . . . $_____ $_____

33 Estimated Equity to Seller (Line 1 less Line 33) . . . . $_____ $_____

34 Less New Contract for Deed to Seller . . . . $_____ $_____

35 Estimated Cash to Seller . . . . $_____ $_____

Seller Two

✔ $210,000 sale price from the full commission, full service comprehensive marketing campaign bringing more buyers to the table

✔ $14,000 7% transaction fee

✔ $196,000 net to seller

Focus on the net amount, which is more a function of sales price than commission rate.

What is the home selling process like and how will it impact their lives?

Here is where you go over the timing of the relationship, the paperwork, and all the steps in the home selling process.

Displace the generalities that people hear in the media and from friends and family with accurate, credible information.

What is the real estate market like?

The best thing you can do to represent the most realistic picture of the market is to be prepared with data and valid, substantive information from respected sources. Displace the generalities that people hear in the media and from friends and family with accurate, credible information that will make you a valued resource for trustworthy information. In real estate, each market—by state, city, neighborhood, and even street—is situation specific, so the conversation should be focused on local conditions.

When working to establish a mutually rewarding and successful relationship, expectations and communication are two essential variables. Discussing the following points in the initial meeting will set the tone for all of the remaining meetings in the sales process. These are the eight variables that determine how quickly and at what price a home will sell:

1. Location—It is what it is; you cannot change it.

2. Condition—That is up to the seller with input from the real estate agent (home preparation and staging).

3. Marketing—That is up to the real estate agent with the seller's counsel (what is the marketing campaign and what aspects of that does the seller want done or not).

4. Seasonality—There are traditionally better times of the year than others to put a home on the market.

5. Interest rates—Not only what they are but whether they are likely to change.

6. Competition—How many and what quality of competing properties are on the market.

7. Market and world conditions—Local and global economies, inflation, recession, terrorism.

8. Price is agreed upon and monitored by the agent and the seller. Price is the easiest variable to alter.

The seller and agent can control condition, marketing, and price.

The seller and agent can control condition, marketing, and price. When a house doesn't sell, look first to the variables you can control. If the seller prepares the property according to the agent's recommendations and you have showings every other day with little to no competition, and if interest rates are great and it is still not selling, look to price as the issue.

If the home is pristine, and all the other variables are in alignment, but showings are poorly attended, the agent's marketing campaign should be reviewed.

Discussing these variables with a client helps cut down on surprises and gives you a shared basis for evaluating strategies. Having this conversation early and often strengthens rapport as well.

Position Yourself

When attempting to secure a listing at some point in the meeting, you will be talking about your marketing campaign. Differentiate yourself from other agents without bad-mouthing them. You can accomplish this by positioning yourself. Essentially, positioning means, "this is how the typical agent markets" and "here is how I do it."

Here is how dialogue may go:

"Mr. and Mrs. Johnson, in a market like this where homes are flying off the market in even a matter of hours versus days, it is imperative to make sure you are still netting the most amount of money out of the sale of your home.

"In my experience, I have learned that in a seller's market many real estate agents will just put a sign in the yard and wait for the home to sell. A week might pass without a sale, so the seller asks the agent what is next. The agent decides to try an Open House that weekend. Nothing. Then they try an ad in the paper. This is a reactive approach to selling and puts the negotiating leverage in the buyer's favor because of extended market time for the listing."

Here is your positioning statement:

"Mr. and Mrs. Johnson, let me explain to you how I would go about selling your home. I use a stacked marketing approach that is designed to create awareness about your property quickly to a targeted audience. I take every component of my comprehensive and well-financed marketing campaign and strategically set it up so all of them hit the market at the same time. I draw from a variety of marketing methods and tools, including internet, mailers to the neighbors, agent box stuffers, and Open Houses. The result is that anyone out there who is a potential candidate for your home will know about it at the end of the initial campaign—so you get more people and more opportunities for more and higher bids. We relentlessly repeat the tactics until we get results. Stacked marketing has focus, so it creates a sense of urgency among buyers."

That conversation alone is the single most compelling story you can tell a seller to secure a listing.

How Does One Prepare the Home For Sale ?

To prepare the home for listing, go through the entire home room by room and make a to-do list for preparing the home for sale. Typically, you will have to prioritize the list to distinguish what absolutely must be done from activities that add only minimal value.

The goal is not to spend $1,000 to get $400 back. The goal is to spend $1,000 to get $5,000 back. Sometimes there are simply things that have to be done whether it returns money to the seller or not— just to get the home sold.

Differentiate yourself from other agents without bad-mouthing them.

When discussing your marketing plans, bring along a calendar that you can provide to the seller. Together, go through the marketing plan components and write them on the calendar. An Open House Sunday 1–4. Write it down. A broker open Tuesday 11–1. Write it down. Make a photocopy so each party has one so the seller can use it as a tool to hold the agent accountable for the game plan.

Assume the sale. Have all the paperwork you need to get a listing up and running. That way, when a prospect is impressed with you and says, "Okay, let's get going!" you won't have to run back to the office for anything. You'll be ready to get going.

Even if your prospect does not want to sign up right away, you can still assume the sale and help your prospect prepare psychologically to sign on with you. Leave disclosure forms to fill out. Provide an "Items needed to sell your home" checklist. Because it is always more difficult for people to **fire** someone than to **hire** someone, make hiring you as easy as you possibly can.

The Buyer's Market

In a seller's market, being a real estate agent is fun and rewarding. You are the hero. But when faced with a large inventory of homes with few motivated buyers, your relationship to your client poses challenges that are best addressed with project management techniques.

Bring along a calendar. Together, go through the marketing plan components and write them on the calendar.

The most common mistake agents make in a relationship where the sell cycle and listing contract of the home takes months instead of days is a failure to communicate. What happens is that even if you are doing everything necessary to get the home sold, the seller doesn't know what you're doing or what impact you're having on the selling process. Sellers who don't hear from you for a few days, even if you have nothing to report, feel abandoned and worry that you are no longer doing anything for them and are no longer passionate about the listing. You combat that by setting up a schedule for communicating. Even if you have no news to share, it's important to check in. Clients have a way of filling voids with all kinds of assumptions that may have no basis in reality. To prevent them from assuming the worst about the market or about you, check in even when there's no news. Letting them know what you have done on their behalf is easy, and it goes a long way toward keeping you and your value top of mind with your client.

Here is how easy it can be to maintain contact and maintain a highly visibility, high-value relationship:

1. Create a communications calendar and stick to it.

2. Provide comprehensive, timely, and accurate feedback about the sales cycle.

3. Provide reports of the activities you have performed and the results of each one. "We had Broker's Open today and had 24 agents through. The comments were very positive as to the condition of the home so thank you and good job. However, there was pretty consistent feedback that the price was about 5% high compared to what they had seen out there."

4. Provide a weekly comprehensive progress report compiling the week's activities and results. Set down the game plan for the coming week's marketing agenda. Talk about the feedback. Do this face-to-face so you can get an accurate read on your client's feelings about progress.

5. Prepare and maintain a mini-comparative market analysis of the activity in the area since going on the market. It gives the client peace of mind when they know they compare with other activity in the market.

6. Provide updates on the marketplace and industry. Statistics, strategies being implemented, trends, and projections all give the client peace of mind.

7. Spell out what you are doing for your client and how you are thinking creatively on their behalf. Even activities that do not sell the home solidify your relationship and keep your reputation intact.

8. Say "thank you" for their loyalty and commitment to you.

In every selling relationship, the bottom line is always to do your best and show the client that you care.

Marketing calendar

Month _____

S	M	Tu	W	Th	F	Sa

COMPARATIVE MARKET ANALYSIS
Similar Properties: SOLD

Category	Subject Property	Comp. #1	Comp. #2	Comp. #3
Address	4517 29th Ave S.	4245 30th Ave S.	4228 32nd Ave S.	4453 33rd Ave S.
Price	TBD	$219,900	$226,000	$223,000
# Bedrooms	3	2	2	2
# Bathrooms	1	1	1	1
Style	1 ½ Stories	1 Story	1 Story	1 ½ Stories
Square Footage	1,170	864	896	1,425
Year Built	1926	1923	1926	1938
Garage	1	1	2	1
Fireplace	Yes	No	No	No
Heat	FA/NG	Gravity/NG	FA/NG	FA/NG
Central Air	No	Window	No	Yes
Taxes	$2,233	$1,671	$1,694	$2,027
Exterior	Stucco	Metal/Vinyl	Stucco	Wood
Location		1 mile	1 mile	1 mile
Condition	Excellent	Excellent	Excellent	Excellent
Below Ground	0	0	0	308
Off Market Date		Pending	4/5/06	3/30/06
Market Time		40 days	86 days	11 days
Appreciation		N/A	N/A	$N/A

COMPARATIVE MARKET ANALYSIS
Similar Properties: Pending

Category	Subject Property	Comp. #1	Comp. #2	Comp. #3
Address	5648 44th Ave. S.	5708 42nd Ave. S.	5600 44th Ave. S.	5605 45th Ave. S.
Price	TBD	$159,900	$184,900	$217,500
# Bedrooms	2	2	3	2
# Bathrooms	1	1	1	1
Style	1 Story	1 Story	1 ½ Stories	1 ½ Stories
Square Footage	1,012	824	1,043	1,102
Year Built	1921	1924	1946	1941
Garage	2	2	2	1
Fireplace	No	No	No	No
Heat	FA/NG	FA/NG	FA/NG	FA/NG
Central Air	Window	Yes	Yes	Yes
Taxes	$1.142	$1,268	$1,419	$1,313
Exterior	Stucco	Wood	Shakes	Metal/Vinyl
Lot	40 X 128	128 X 43	40 X 128	40 X 128
Location		1 mile	1 mile	1 mile
Condition	Good	Good	Good	Good
Below Ground	200	0	0	352
Off Market Date		2/9/04	1/30/04	2/11/04
Market Time		7 days	5 days	14 days
Appreciation		$161,499	$186,749	$219,675

COMPARATIVE MARKET ANALYSIS
Similar Properties: For Sale

Category	Subject Property	Comp. #1	Comp. #2	Comp. #3
Address	11409 Oakvale Rd. S.	5410 Holiday Rd.	11701 Karen Ln.	11401 Oakvale Rd. N.
Price	TBD	$239,900	$254,900	$259,900
# Bedrooms	3	4	3	3
# Bathrooms	2	2	2	2
Style	1 Story	1 Story	Split Entry	2 Stories
Square Footage	1,552	1,713	1,943	1,816
Year Built	1954	1957	1963	1918
Garage	2	1	2	2
Fireplace	Yes	Yes	No	Yes
Heat	FA/NG	FA/NG	HW/NG	FA/NG
Central Air	Yes	Yes	Wall	Yes
Taxes	$2,270	$2,207	$1,552	$2,388
Exterior	Wood	Wood	Shakes, Stucco	Wood
Location		1 mile	1 mile	1 mile
Condition		Good	Good	Good
Below Ground	0	585	793	0
Off Market Date				
Market Time				
Appreciation				

Listing Checklist

[P R O P E R T Y]

- ☐ Initial meeting
- ☐ Thank you to client
- ☐ Thank you to referral source
- ☐ Paperwork filled out
- ☐ Order virtual tour
- ☐ Create file
- ☐ Add to Clients in Progress
- ☐ Add to Sales Pro
- ☐ Disclosures copied (25), Binder made
- ☐ Truth in sale of housing (10)
- ☐ Loan payoff
- ☐ Abstract
- ☐ Copy to client of paperwork
- ☐ Turn in file to listing coordinator (Agency, Listing Contract, Input)
- ☐ Review for accuracy
- ☐ Load photos
- ☐ Real estate agent Showcase of Homes
- ☐ Add to Sell My Home
- ☐ Lockbox (code)
- ☐ Create brochures
- ☐ ½ page for Brochure Box; full page, 2-sided, for property

- ☐ Full page announcing Brokers Open
- ☐ ½ page for neighborhood mailer
- ☐ Print brochures
- ☐ Deliver signage
- ☐ Brochure Box
- ☐ Hotline text, voice, and visual
- ☐ Sell My Home
- ☐ Feedback
- ☐ Home Docs
- ☐ Networking
- ☐ MLS and Internet
- ☐ Star Tribune.com
- ☐ Target marketing e-mail
- ☐ Local paper advertising
- ☐ Network One
- ☐ Warranty program
- ☐ Office Networking
- ☐ Schedule Broker's Open
- ☐ Deliver brochure box, lockbox, brochures, TISH, binder, seller's disclosures, signs
- ☐ E-mail sphere
- ☐ Set up Open House
- ☐ Star Tribune four color

- ☐ Once "SOLD," notify front desk
- ☐ Put out "SOLD" sign
- ☐ Turn in file
- ☐ If different closing company than Edina Title, make sure copy goes to closer
- ☐ Copy client
- ☐ Send moving kit to client
- ☐ File for folder
- ☐ Determine appraisal value is complete
- ☐ Assure title work is on-going
- ☐ Notify client of status at all times
- ☐ Confirm walk-through
- ☐ Confirm preparation for closing complete with client
- ☐ Remove lockbox and personal sign/name rider
- ☐ Closing
- ☐ Change new address on client list
- ☐ Vacant homes
- ☐ Winterize/de-winterize home
- ☐ Order lawn care, snow removal
- ☐ Check on home periodically

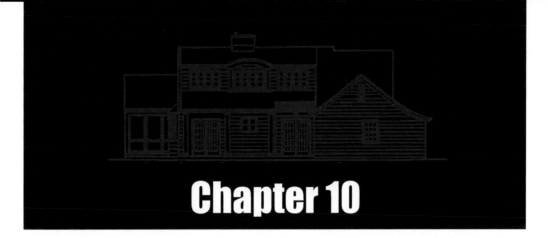

Chapter 10

It's Understanding Both Sides of the Street

"The true test of a great real estate agent is leaving their client neither out on the street or doubled up on mortgage payments."

—Accomplished Real Estate Agent

One of the most challenging yet rewarding opportunities in real estate is to demonstrate to your clients that you can help them sell their home, purchase a new one, *and* assist them with the transition from one to the other—across the street or across the country. Your goal is to avoid leaving them out on the street or doubled up on mortgage payments.

Begin by doing a market analysis on the existing home to determine the probable time frame for selling it. Start with the same eight factors we discussed in chapter eight:

1 Marketing

2 Location

3 Condition

4 Interest rates

5 Competition

6 Seasonality

7 Market/world conditions

8 Price

Next enter search criteria for your client's ideal home *purchase* and determine which and how many of the homes that meet their criteria sold in the last year. If six homes that meet their criteria sold last year, you may be in for a long search as that is essentially one home sold every two months. If on the other hand 120 homes sold, or one every three days, the likelihood of finding one your client will like is very good.

Writing contingent is typically the least attractive alternative because if sellers feel they have the upper hand due to the contingency, they can compromise the buyer's ability to negotiate.

If salability factors on your client's home are strong and there are several buying options for your clients to choose from, writing contingent may be a viable strategy. But if it looks like selling is going to take some time and choices on a purchase are slim, it would make more sense to sell the existing home first and get "freed up" so when the right home does come on the market, your client is ready to move on it.

Writing contingent is typically the least attractive alternative because if sellers feel they have the upper hand due to the contingency, they can compromise the buyer's ability to negotiate. Even financially disciplined clients who are selling contingent can cave on price, terms, and conditions when an offer comes in because they feel at the mercy of the offer to make things happen to get the property they are seeking to purchase. Therefore, when meeting with the contingent client, you should be prepared with options for temporary housing and storage facilities in case you need it for that "in between homes" period.

If indeed your client decides to write contingencies, you can proactively reduce the stress for everyone and still make the contingent offer attractive in the eyes of the seller. First, have your client prepare the home for sale with all the usual walkthrough consultations and to-do lists. Do a market analysis to show the salability of your client's home. If the statistics show that there is very little to no competition and that the market time for homes selling in that area is very low in terms of days, then when presenting the offer to the listing agent of the home your clients want to buy, you can show them that your client's home is likely to sell quickly because of its price and your marketing strategy. That pro-active approach to having the home ready to go to market increases the likelihood of a quick sale, thereby making all parties more confident in a quick sale for your client, who can then make their new purchase.

Next, prepare the listing paperwork and a marketing plan for your client's property to show the listing agent and build confidence that you are proactively prepared to go to market should the listing agent's client take the offer. Show the listing agent your marketing plan and statistics indicating that your homes' average market times are low to increase confidence in your ability to sell the home quickly.

Next, have all your marketing materials on your client's home—including brochures, pictures, home highlights, and updates—to once again gain their confidence in the salability of the home. You may even have them visit the home. Keep in mind, conversely, if you are a listing agent considering a contingent offer, these are all of the details you should expect before accepting a contingent offer to protect your client's best interests.

Finally, the overall market conditions determine the probability of contingent offers being acceptable. In a seller's market, contingent offers are much more commonly accepted. Conversely, in a market when homes are not selling very well, contingent offers are less attractive. Therefore, the buyer selling a home first may be the only option.

If someone is an incoming buyer, provide them with information that makes assimilating into the new environment much easier, like school and tax information, and "Welcome Wagon" materials, as they are not just moving from one home to another, but from one lifestyle to another.

If someone is an incoming buyer, provide them with information that makes assimilating into the new environment much easier.

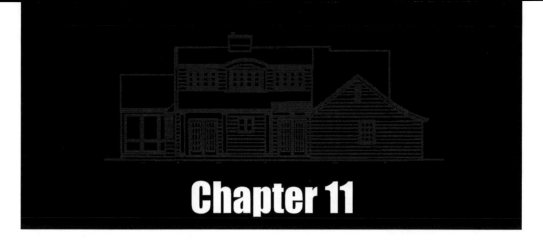

Chapter 11

It's an E-business

"I use to think that cyberspace was fifty years away.
What I thought was fifty years away, was only ten years away.
And what I thought was ten years away . . . it was already here.
I just wasn't aware of it yet."

—Bruce Sterling

Attracting the Gen-Y Client

Real estate as we know it has gone through more changes in the last three years than the previous thirty. Much of this is a result of the innumerable changes in technology combined with the changing profile of real estate agents and changing consumer behavior. Technology has been instrumental in changing the abilities and the mindset of today's consumer as they now can expect and obtain instantaneous and free online access to all kinds of information that only agents used to possess.

Remember the days of driving across town to deliver a purchase agreement or wanting to make a telephone call but having to wait to get to

your office to use a telephone? And long gone are the days of looking through a telephone book-sized listing directory with postage-stamp-size pictures and a paragraph-length description of properties.

In reality, however, the Web makes our lives easier.

Along came cellular phones and fax machines as the new way of conducting transactions. Next came the computer and life as we knew it would never be the same. Whether all the technology changes are for better or worse for the profession is a matter of whether you fight it or embrace it.

What scares many agents is that the once-sacred proprietary information via the multiple listing service is now readily available to the general public. Agents who want their clients to be tethered to them for information lose that advantage and have to live with the fear that clients no longer need them.

In reality, however, the Web makes our lives easier. By making more information available to buyers, the Web can reduce the average number of homes a buyer wants to see from twenty to six. Who is the beneficiary of time management when *that* happens?

Consumers want information that enables them to make good decisions. Fortunately for agents, clients still have to get into homes to see them, feel them, smell them, and touch them to know which house is right for them. We still hold the keys to the house.

Welcome to the Y-Generation! Their life is one of iPods, MySpace, Game Cubes, text messaging, and cell phones starting at age six and seven. What that means for today's real estate agent is that to be a provider of information is no longer enough. In fact, to provide

To provide goods and services is no longer enough, as consumers now expect valuable experiences.

goods and services is no longer enough, as consumers now expect ***valuable experiences.***

They look to us not for information—they can get a lot of that themselves. They look to us for wisdom, methods for saving them time and money, and the latest in real estate trends, home construction technology, school systems, transportation system outlooks, population growth areas, and negotiation and representation sills. They want the expert counsel it takes to make informed decisions. To attain and maintain the expertise that's in demand increases our need to invest in technology, continuing education, salesmanship, and self-improvement. Agents must read newsletters, industry periodicals, and the latest statistics on the market to do justice to ourselves and our clients. By providing clients with meaningful experiences that match dreams to the homes that fulfill them, we bring value to the equation and remain at the center of the relationship.

Defining tools of the real-estate agent

Home Docs

Sites like homedocs.com and others track all aspects of a client's real estate transaction throughout the selling/buying process and leave a web-based paper trail. The system enables the client to keep track of the transaction, which delivers valuable peace of mind.

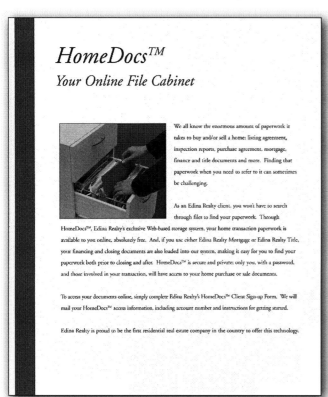

Virtual tour

A virtual, video-based tour of a property is more than just a still photo; it allows your client to get a truer feeling for the home by showing a 360-degree view of each main space. Virtual tours significantly reduce the amount of time needed to find a home.

Sell My Home

A user-friendly on-line tool that lets the client monitor all aspects of the selling of the home from showing activity, feedback, and marketing recap information to name a few.

The client is no longer totally dependent on the communication with the agent for the activity and progress of the selling process as it is accessible 24/7 via computer.

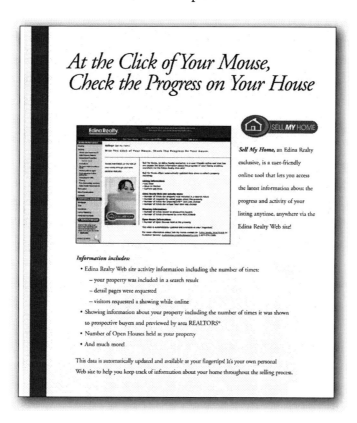

Mobile property listing technology

Clients can now not only receive verbal descriptions of the homes from For-Sale sign information but also download and view pictures and multiple listing information right to their PDAs. The technology allows instant gratification and information for a client to see whether they want to delve further into the property.

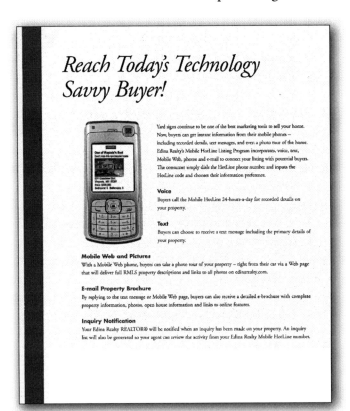

Advanced digital cameras

A good camera enables you to get high-quality shots of properties for your website, for e-mailing, and for brochure design and MLS input.

Laptops and mobile printers

A computer and printer make your world essentially virtual. You can be out and about while doing business and not be tethered to an office computer. You can be more accessible to clients and others you need to be with to develop and maintain business.

PDA devices

These lap-top computers the size of a cell phone offer many benefits of a lap top with the advantage of being much more compact.

Satellite imagery: See Google Earth

You can see aerial views of homes and the surrounding areas to assess their appeal to clients. Look for proximity to train tracks, commercial buildings, and highways, to save yourself and your client time and money wasted on visiting the wrong properties.

MySpace & YouTube Technologies are computer-based ways of communicating and advertising.

The client of today uses this media mode to stay in touch with everything happening.

Software programs

There are a myriad of software programs to help both the real estate agent and client. They save time, money, and stress, and help both get the most out of the transaction and relationship.

A computer and printer make your world essentially virtual.

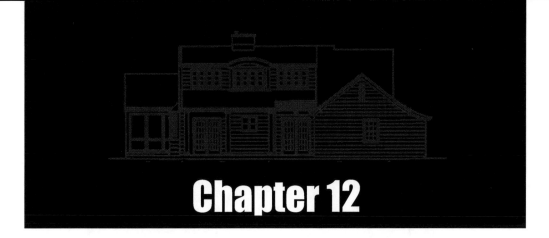

Chapter 12

It's an Open House that Never Closes

"It wasn't raining when Noah built the ark."

—Howard Ruff

Holding an *effective* Open House.

Note the emphasis on "effective" Open House. When investing the time, energy, and money to hold an Open House, do you have the proper mindset with goals for the open or are you going through the motions of holding it open to appease your seller? The ultimate goal of an Open House should be to represent the seller and do what you can to sell the home with price, terms, and conditions in the seller's best interest. But the truth of the matter is that an Open House can also be an effective way of attaining buyers in the marketplace. Though agent representation for buyers is more common than it used to be, there are still a large number of buyers out there wondering around without an agent.

The time you spend before and after the event are as important as the time you spend at the event.

The time you spend before and after the event are as important as the time you spend at the event. Like the rest of this business, you can talk to ten agents and find ten different ways of holding an open, but the bottom line is that you have to do what feels comfortable for you. You have to decide whether to make everybody sign in and then call them back or not have them sign in and pursue one or two people with whom to build rapport on the spot.

The following are tips for holding a successful Open House:

- ✔ Know why you **believe** in the home and what you plan to say about it
- ✔ Hold an Open House where you want to make a name for yourself; work where you play for greater **visibility**
- ✔ Decide whether you want quantity or quality. Find a strategic **location** with high visibility and traffic to reach a large number of people or a more remote location with fewer people that may lead to a higher quality dialogue with prospective clients
- ✔ A **price point** with which you are comfortable, i.e., first-time homebuyers versus upper-bracket homes
- ✔ Work a price point where you can get someone who is looking to buy also needs a place to sell so you get **double the business**

Take time during the week before the Open House to preview the neighborhood and competing properties.

Now that you have determined the home and area, it is time to go to work. It is important to know about the neighborhood and its profile in terms of children, schools, religious institutions, distance to transportation systems, shopping, restaurants, and amenities like parks and lakes.

Take time during the week before the Open House to preview the neighborhood and competing properties so when asked, you can answer questions knowledgably. The Multiple Listing Service will tell you the "solds, pendings, offmarkets" and so forth so you can present yourself as the local area specialist and expert in the field.

During the week prior, make address labels for homes in the area inviting the neighbors to the Open House. Many neighbors want nothing more than to finally get into those homes but are embarrassed to come as they feel they will be perceived as the "nosey neighbors" when in fact they are very helpful in bringing buyers to the listing. How many times have visitors told you they are looking on behalf of a friend or family member?

You may want to go so far as having a "special Open House" for the neighbors on Saturday so they feel special. It is a great way to obtain them as possible listings as well due to the more subdued, less inhibited nature of the people attending as they were invited to be there.

Schedule the time of the Open House to avoid conflicting with other attention getters like sporting events or community activities.

On the actual day of the Open House, allow yourself plenty of time to get to the property so you are not rushed.

On the actual day of the Open House, allow yourself plenty of time to get to the property so you are not rushed. Buyers standing on the front steps waiting ten minutes prior to the scheduled open to be the first ones in may be the best and most motivated buyers. Plus being there early shows you are focused, are disciplined, and plan well should they be looking for an agent.

One way to gain exposure for the Open House and please your seller is to present a comprehensive and well-financed marketing campaign instead of merely running a free ad in a newspaper. An effective agent runs an ad in the Saturday and Sunday newspaper for a Sunday Open House, and in the case of the Twin Cities markets for example, both the Minneapolis and St. Paul newspapers. Needless to say, with the changing demographics and home search processes of the new buyer out there, the internet is a more prevalent way to find Open Houses these days, so having an online presence is essential.

When writing the ad, word it to highlight its unique advantages. Instead of listing obvious features like "3 bedroom, 2 bathroom," put "First Open House," "Great location," or "Immaculate Condition."

Place plenty of signs to attract buyers and get exposure for you and your business. The key is to be professional and discretionary about the number of signs you put out.

Take the flyers out of the brochure box if one exists to prevent people from looking at the price and walking away. People have to get into a home, smell it, touch it, and experience it to determine its true value.

Open houses are always a matter of style. Many people have soft music and food aromas going to create an ambiance and welcoming feeling.

Take the flyers out of the brochure box if one exists to prevent people from looking at the price and walking away.

In addition to a brochure about the property, it can be extremely beneficial to have "Solds" in the area, information about other properties for sale nearby, a personal brochure, an actual buyer packet on the home-buying process, real estate trends, and appreciation rates. Especially useful is a list of properties coming up on the market that you know about through your company's network, showing you have the inside track on the market place, which can be of benefit to the buyers.

But before any of this can be done to be legally compliant, your agency relationship must be disclosed in one form or another to the general public attending the Open House. Putting in a clear acrylic stand at the entry featuring your agency relationship is a must.

To whom, when, what, and how you provide material is a matter of personal preference. In my experience, it works to treat an Open House like a party and be the host who makes sure guests are looked after.

Another tip is to do what you can to bring lower the initial barriers and eliminate consumer's red flags. This is key because people have stereotypes about real estate agents and want nothing more than to be left alone. I typically do not stand right in the doorway for that reason.

Always introduce yourself and welcome visitors. "Welcome, and thanks for coming. I realize you are here to see the property so feel free to look around, and my name is Jim if you have any questions."

Asking visitors how they heard about the home is important because you will learn which of your marketing efforts are working. You will also learn whether they are tire kickers or serious buyers who have sought out the property. Finally, it's a good question to ask an initial open-ended question initiating conversation and dialogue. It can also determine whether they are working with an agent, as most of the time that is when they tell you.

As a service to your seller and the home you are representing, present the home in its best light. Make a note of a few features or benefits that might not be obvious. For example, dialogue might be—

> "I would like to point out that there is a door to the attic that could lead to a converted fourth level of the home. Let me show you where that is."

As you walk with them to that door you can then start asking open-ended questions that originate some dialogue. Walking with someone side-by-side is a compelling non-verbal way of getting on the same wavelength with them.

To keep the conversation going, avoid asking yes/no question like this: "Have you seen a lot out there today?"

Instead, ask open-ended questions that require a more thorough response: "What do you think of what you have seen?" "How does it compare to this home?" "How do you feel about the inventory out there?"

It can be fruitful to find out how they are feeling because if they are frustrated by the search, you may be able to help them with your services.

"Did you know that only a small percentage of homes on the market are actually advertised as available?" With the advent of the internet, more and more people now know the inventory, but they don't know how to get into it unless they have an agent, and if they don't, that is where you come in. A very effective technique is to have a laptop loaded and running on an island in the kitchen where you can direct them and say, "Have you seen this property? It is in the area and in a similar price." Show them enough about that one and others to tickle their fancy enough to say, "Yes, we would like to get into that one." That's when you come to the rescue—after, that is, you have determined they are not interested in the Open House property and are not represented by another agent. Respecting relationships legally, morally, and ethically is paramount in running a successful business.

Always have your top five questions ready to ask.

Always have your top five questions ready to ask. Below is a list of possible "icebreaker" questions:

- ✔ Did you find the property in an ad, signs, or the Internet?
- ✔ What do you think about this home?
- ✔ How does it compare to others you have seen today?
- ✔ What exactly are looking for in a home?
- ✔ Have you seen the home over on ……?
- ✔ Would you like to get into that home?

If you point out properties that compete with your listing, do so only after you have determined that the subject listing is not an option. Otherwise you will have an upset seller when the neighbor comes through and overhears a conversation in which you present other opportunities to buyers in their home. Diplomacy, tact and discretion are the better part of business when holding an Open House.

When handing out any sort of information, print at a minimum your contact information on the back so prospective clients can contact you. Highlight where it appears on documents. Best case scenario is that you have a mini-brochure or a DVD on yourself.

Always express your desire to help in any way you can, and if you get contact information follow-up, follow-up, follow-up—as you will probably be the only one who does and that may be what they are looking for in the end.

And finally, worst-case scenario—If you have a very slow Open House, use that time to relax and read a book, work on the computer, or do those administrative activities you ordinarily avoid because you don't make time to do them.

Attract buyers to your Open House with these must-haves

- ✔ Easel to display information
- ✔ Comparable active and sold properties in the area
- ✔ Interest rate sheet
- ✔ Lender promotions
- ✔ School and neighborhood news and information
- ✔ Pre-list properties forthcoming on the market
- ✔ Home Buyer's Scorecard (a brochure that allows you to write notes on opens you have been through)
- ✔ Give aways (pens, calendars, hats)
- ✔ Agency Representation Disclosure
- ✔ Appreciation tables of the various areas
- ✔ A laptop
- ✔ Personal brochure of yourself and company
- ✔ New listings
- ✔ A drawing for a prize
- ✔ A positive attitude!

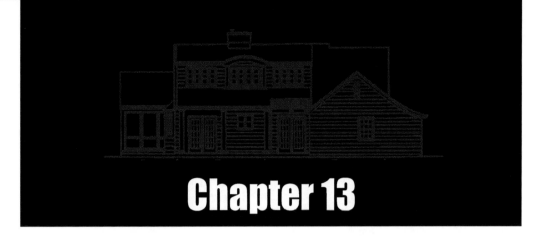

Chapter 13

It's Financial Management

"Why is there so much month at the end of the money."

—Anonymous

A critical part of your business plan is financial planning for the business. A major attraction to the business of being a real estate agent is the opportunity for unlimited income and if successful, some of the best earnings of any career. But if your financial situation is not properly managed, it can become a runaway train and your business will suffer. The earliest mistake many agents make is creating problems with the IRS because they have no method of managing income and taxes every pay period. The solution is a sound accounting system.

If your financial situation is not properly managed, it can become a runaway train and your business will suffer.

When working for most traditional corporate companies, you get a net pay check with social security and federal and state income taxes withheld for you. As a real estate agent, you get a wonderful $12,000 check and the tendency is to think that this is what you have to spend. But of course, it's not all yours. You have to deduct taxes and social security and unemployment insurance. A financial projection for the year will show you how much money you actually have to work with. The projection forces you to make forecasts about income and to account for deductions. With a yearlong—or better still, a two-year projection—you will be able to show seasonal fluctuations and the impact of increased expenses or sales before you get into hot water.

Projections help with cash flow. One month you may earn $26,000 and then nothing for the next three months—then another $40,000 and then nothing for two months. It is the easiest way in the world to get into trouble; something termed a false sense of financial position.

It's not what you earn but what you spend that can make or break you.

Projections include expenses that have to come out of our income, so you can use them to set up personal and business budgets that are the basis for the rest of your financial planning. Factor in a "discretionary expense" part of the budget. It is not the monthly fixed mortgage or car and insurance payments that become the problem. It is the vacations, the trips to the mall, and the children's school expenses that become the unbudgeted items that create the problem.

BUSINESS EXPENSES FOR THE YEAR 2008

	JAN	FEB	MAR	APR	MAY	JUN	JUL	AUG	SEP	OCT	NOV	DEC	TOTAL
Accounting Fees													0
Advertising/Marketing Expense													0
Auto/AAA													0
Bank Charges													0
Commissions Paid													0
Dues & Publications													0
Direct TV													0
Delivery & Freight													0
Employee Benefits													0
Gifts & Tickets													0
Insurance													0
Interest (Banks, etc.)													0
Internet Expense													0
Laundry & Cleaning													0
Legal & Professional													0
Licenses & Permits													0
Meals & Entertainment													0
Miscellaneous													0
Office Supplies/Expenses													0
Outside Services/Contractors													0
Parking & Tolls													0
Pensions & Profit-Sharing													0
Postage													0
Printing													0
Professional Development													0
Profit													0
Rent/Lease Expense													0
Repairs													0
Security Expense													0
Supplies													0
Taxes- Real Estate													0
Taxes-Payroll/Other													0
Telephone													0
Tools													0
Travel													0
Uniforms													0
Utilities													0
Corporate Trip													0
Web													0
Total													0
Wages													0
Corporate 2% Marketing													0
Total	0	0	0	0	0	0	0	0	0	0	0	0	0
Grand Total	0	0	0	0	0	0	0	0	0	0	0	0	0

Use the following categories to create a useful budget:

- ✔ Personal expenses
- ✔ Taxes
- ✔ Investments
- ✔ Mortgage
- ✔ Car payments
- ✔ Insurance
- ✔ Food
- ✔ Gasoline
- ✔ Utilities
- ✔ College education
- ✔ Spending money/allowance
- ✔ Children's school and athletic activities
- ✔ Extra buffer money for unforeseen expenses
- ✔ Business expenses
- ✔ Marketing budget-mailers
- ✔ Printing costs
- ✔ Signs for Open Houses
- ✔ Technology devices
- ✔ Dues and subscriptions
- ✔ Continuing education
- ✔ Errors and omissions dues
- ✔ Multiple listing service dues
- ✔ Company expenses

Depending on the company you work for, you may be able to have these payments deducted into separate accounts for easier accounting. If not, the best thing to do is to create accounts with either your local bank or with your financial planner. In your plan, set up business accounts separate from your personal accounts to keep your business expenses separate for accounting and tax purposes. As for saving, many go as far as to set up three separate accounts: one for short-term investments, one for long-term investments, and one for liquid cash.

Creating projections that account for business income and expenses helps you spend wisely, keep current with your bills, and gain some control over fluctuations in income.

Set up business accounts separate from your personal accounts to keep your business expenses separate for accounting and tax purposes.

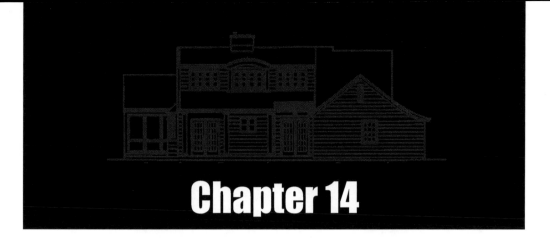

Chapter 14

And at the End of the Day...

"The happiness of a man in this life does not consist in the absence but in the mastery of his passions."

—Alfred Lord Tennyson

You can read this book, practice the exercises, attend continuing education classes, listen to CDs and watch DVDs, attend seminars, and get advanced credentials through more education. You can be the hardest working and most skilled real estate agent in the industry.

After all of that, if you truly, sincerely, and passionately do not redefine yourself in terms of your client's best interests, then the sun will go down on your business.

The brighter tomorrow begins when you redefine yourself as a client-oriented real estate agent always on the lookout for new ways to serve the people who matter most to your business.

Index

F

feature-and-benefit statements, 47

features, 57

federal income taxes, 153–54

feedback

    during property visits, 100–101

    from trial closes, 48–50

fees, ix–x, 20, 117–19

financial information, 98

financial planning

    advantages of, 153–54

    expenses and, 20, 154–55

    projections for, 154–57

    tool for, 20

fliers, 145, 147

follow-up, 40, 56

G

goals

    for activities, 16

    annual, 8, 9

    in daily to-do list, 8, 12

    establishing interest in, 45, 59

    of home buyers, x

    long-term, 6–7

    as manageable tasks, 13

    purpose of, 5

    quarterly, 8, 10

    weekly, 11

Google Earth, 141

H

holiday letters, 79–81

home buyers

    assessment of, 101

    checklist for, 110

    education of, 35, 54–55

    goals of, x

    information usage and, x

    letters for, 75–76, 78–79, 87–88

    mindset of, viii, 135

    time management and, 136

    See also clients; prospective customers

home checklists, 100–101

home sellers

    expectations of, 111–12

    letters for, 75–79, 81–83, 90

    meetings with, 112–21

home-buying process

    pre-approvals, 98, 105

    purchase agreements, 101–4

    walk-through process, 107–8

    See also closings

HomeDocs, 138

home-selling process

    explanation of, 119

    offers, 88, 103–6

    preparation of homes in, 115–16, 122–23

    purchase agreements, 101–4

    See also selling process

HUD (Housing and Urban Development), 108–9

I

icebreaker questions, 150

impressions, 64, 66

incentives, 34

income, 2–3, 154

income taxes, 153–54

independence, 2

information, x–xi, 135–36, 149

inspections, 106–7

itineraries, 28–29, 31

L

laptops, 140

lawsuits, 106

leads, ix–x

lenders, 98

Praise for
Real Estate Agent Redefined

"There are all kinds of resources for the real estate industry, but this is the one book that is a real nuts and bolts, A–Z guide to running a successful business."

—Chris, Real Estate Trainer and Coach—

"Since implementing the system of delegating out the tasks that I do not like to do or am not good at, I find I have more energy and passion while in front of my clients—something they do notice. And referrals are up as a result."

—Kristen, Sales Associate, **Fortune 500 Company—**

"By incorporating "The Selling Process" into my presentations, I now have to meet with fewer potential prospects to get the same or more clients to come on service with me because of my increased close ratio."

—Larry, Real Estate Agent—

"It is amazing how I knew so many of the things I was supposed to be doing, but the concepts in this program of setting up habits and disciplines created consistency and operations as a part of my business. I never thought prospecting could be so easy."

—Elizabeth, First Year Agent—

"I never thought I could work less and earn more money by simply customizing my marketing materials and corporate identification program with a more sophisticated look and in turn doubling my average sales price by working with higher end clients. It was the perception that this was the market I served through my upscale branding image."

—John, Distinctive Homes Estate Agent—

"The quality of my personal life has been greatly improved, and I have found a more work/play balance that was always difficult to accomplish in this business of real estate. Incorporating the concept of different days for different things in my life, I learned to plan my months out in advance on the calendar, which resulted in spending more time with my family and friends without sacrificing any client service."

—Kim, Certified Real Estate Specialist—